FTCE Elementary Education K–6 (060) Subtest 4: Mathematics (604) Study Guide

Dear Educator,

Welcome to Teacher Preps, and thank you for purchasing this study guide!

Best of luck on your exam!
TeacherPreps Team

50% OFF our online test prep!

Ensure you get a passing score on test day by giving yourself the all-access test prep, which includes online practice tests, video lessons, and interactive vocabulary exercises!

1. Visit this link: https://prep.thrivecart.com/teacher-preps/

2. Enter **50OFFPREP** in the coupon code

3. Take the full-length practice test to check if you're ready for test day!

Strategy and Test Tips:

The Ultimate Guide for Your Teacher Certification Exam

When preparing for your exam, review these study tips to have a higher chance of success on test day!

Understanding Exam Structure and Content

Learn What the Exam Covers

- **Review our study guide**: Start by thoroughly reading the guide for your exam, focusing on the overview and exam framework to understand the content areas.

- **Assess Your Knowledge**: Identify which areas you need to focus on based on your familiarity and confidence with the material.

Familiarize Yourself with Question Types

When preparing for your teacher certification exam, you'll encounter various types of questions designed to assess different aspects of your knowledge and skills. Here's a breakdown of the most common types you'll see:

Multiple-Choice Questions (MCQs)

- **Structure**: Typically consists of a question or statement (the stem) followed by several answer choices.

- **Strategy**: Read the stem carefully, eliminate clearly wrong answers, and choose the best option among the remaining choices. Remember, there's no penalty for guessing, so it's in your best interest to answer every question.

Constructed Response Questions

- **Structure**: These require you to construct your own answer rather than selecting from provided options. This could be in the form of short answers, essays, or other written formats.

- **Strategy**: Make sure to address all parts of the prompt clearly and comprehensively. Organize your thoughts before writing and review your answers to ensure they are complete and on topic.

Case Studies and Scenario-Based Questions

- **Structure**: These present a realistic situation or problem that you might face in a classroom setting, asking you to apply your knowledge to solve a problem or propose a strategy.

- **Strategy**: Carefully analyze the scenario to understand all elements involved before proposing a solution. Ensure your answer is grounded in theoretical knowledge and practical applicability.

Data Analysis Questions

- **Structure**: These may involve interpreting data from charts, graphs, or tables to answer questions based on the analysis.

- **Strategy**: Focus on understanding how to read various data presentations and practice calculating and drawing conclusions from provided data.

Effective Study Strategies

Develop a Study Plan

- **Create a Personalized Schedule**: Set up a study schedule that suits your individual learning pace and timeline.
- **Focus on Weak Areas**: Prioritize studying areas where you feel less confident.

Test Preparation and Taking Tips

Before the Exam

- **Plan Your Study Time**: Avoid cramming by planning your study time well ahead of the exam date.
- **Practice Regularly**: Make use of practice tests and sample questions to build confidence and familiarity with the exam format.

On Exam Day

- **Be Prepared**: Ensure you know the location and logistics of the test center. Arrive early, well-rested, and have a good meal beforehand.
- **Dress Comfortably**: Wear layers for adjustable comfort, regardless of the room temperature.

During the Exam

- **Read Questions Carefully**: Pay close attention to what each question is asking, especially the wording.
- **Manage Your Time**: Keep track of time and pace yourself to ensure you can answer all questions.

- **Guess Strategically**: There is no penalty for wrong answers, so make educated guesses if unsure.

Smart Tips for Success

- **No Trick Questions**: Focus on the straightforward request of each question without looking for hidden meanings.

- **Use All Available Time**: If finished early, review your answers, especially those you are unsure about.

After the Exam

- **Reflect on Your Performance**: Assess which areas were challenging and focus future studies on these.

Are You Ready?

- **Final Checklist**: Before the test day, ensure you understand all exam requirements, have practiced sufficiently, and are familiar with the question types and test strategies.

By following these guidelines, you will be well-prepared to tackle your teacher certification exam. Remember, effective preparation is the key to success. Good luck!

About the Exam

Aspect	Details
Exam Name	Elementary Education K–6
Exam Code	60
Topics	Subtest 1: Language Arts and Reading (601) Subtest 2: Social Science (602) Subtest 3: Science (603) Subtest 4: Mathematics (604)
Duration	Subtest 1: 1 hour and 5 minutes Subtest 2: 1 hour and 5 minutes Subtest 3: 1 hour and 10 minutes Subtest 4: 1 hour and 10 minutes
Question Count	Subtest 1: 50 multiple-choice questions Subtest 2: 45 multiple-choice questions Subtest 3: 45 multiple-choice questions Subtest 4: 35 multiple-choice questions
Test Format	Computer-administered test (CAT)
Passing Score	Examinees must score at least 200 per subtest, and pass all 4 subtests to pass this exam.

# Test Prep Checklist

FTCE Elementary Education K–6 (060) Subtest 4: Mathematics (604) Study Guide

Track your preparation progress with this checklist!

Lesson	Date	Status
Strategy and Test Tips		
Mathematics Instruction		
Number Concepts and Operations		
Patterns and Algebra		
Geometry and Measurement		
Probability and Statistics		
Mathematics Practice Test: • https://www.teacherpreps.com/elementary-mathematics-test		

Subtest 4: Mathematics

Topic	Percentage of Total Subtest Questions
Knowledge of integers, decimals, and fractions in base-10	29%
Knowledge of algebraic reasoning	15%
Knowledge of measurement, data analysis, and statistics	14%
Knowledge of geometric concepts	15%
Knowledge of student reasoning and instructional practices	27%

Online Practice Tests:

- **Mathematics Practice Test**:
  https://www.teacherpreps.com/elementary-mathematics-test

Mathematics Instruction

Introduction

Mathematics, more than just a system of numbers and symbols, plays a pivotal role in helping students develop critical thinking, problem-solving abilities, and a logical mindset. Your exam seeks to ensure that educators possess the foundational knowledge and practical understanding needed to effectively teach these skills. At the heart of this endeavor is Mathematics Instruction.

Mathematics instruction revolves around an educator's comprehension of how students acquire mathematical abilities and how this understanding informs their instructional choices.

In essence, this mathematics instruction assesses:

- **Understanding of Mathematical Learning**: Recognizing cognitive processes and developmental stages in which students absorb and process mathematical information.
- **Instructional Planning**: Designing strategies and selecting resources that cater to diverse learning styles and needs, ensuring that mathematical concepts are accessible to all students.
- **Organizing and Implementing Instruction**: Structuring lessons that foster an interactive, engaging, and conducive environment for mathematical exploration and understanding.
- **Assessment**: Employing a range of evaluation tools to gauge students' grasp of the subject matter, identifying areas of strength and addressing gaps in understanding.

To be effective mathematics educators, it's crucial to meld content knowledge with instructional best practices. Math instruction underscores this fusion, emphasizing the importance of meeting students where they are and guiding them towards mathematical mastery. As we cover this study guide, we'll unpack the various aspects of math instruction, equipping you with the knowledge and strategies you'll need to excel in both the examination and the classroom.

Research-based Theories and Principles of Learning Mathematics

The process of learning mathematics is a complex blend of cognitive development, conceptual understanding, procedural skill, and practice. To ensure all students reach their maximum potential in mathematics, educators must be well-versed in the research-based theories and principles that guide effective instruction.

1. Constructivist Theory:

Description: Proposes that learners construct knowledge based on their experiences. Instead of passively receiving information, students actively create their understanding, building upon what they already know.

Implication for Teaching: Offer hands-on tasks and problem-solving activities. Encourage students to explore, question, and discuss mathematical concepts.

2. Sociocultural Theory (Vygotsky):

Description: Learning is deeply embedded within social interactions. Through collaboration and dialogue, more experienced individuals can guide learners.

Implication for Teaching: Incorporate group work and collaborative projects. Use "scaffolding" techniques to provide temporary support to students as they develop new skills.

3. Zone of Proximal Development (ZPD):

Description: A concept also by Vygotsky, ZPD represents the difference between what learners can do without help and what they can achieve with guidance.

Implication for Teaching: Identify each student's ZPD and offer the right level of challenge. Adjust instructional support as students progress.

4. Cognitive Load Theory:

Description: Proposes that the brain's working memory has a limited capacity. Overloading it with excessive information or confusing stimuli can hinder learning.

Implication for Teaching: Break complex topics into smaller chunks. Use visuals, manipulatives, and real-life examples to make abstract concepts more tangible.

5. Mastery Learning (Bloom):

Description: Argues that all students can understand material, provided they get appropriate learning conditions and time.

Implication for Teaching: Use formative assessments to identify areas of struggle. Provide feedback and additional time or resources for students to master challenging topics.

Strategies for Planning Appropriate Instructional Activities:

Differentiated Instruction: Tailor teaching methods to cater to diverse learning styles, readiness levels, and interests. For instance, visual learners might benefit from diagrams while kinesthetic learners prefer hands-on activities.

Use of Manipulatives: Physical tools, like blocks or interactive digital platforms, can provide tangible experiences for abstract mathematical concepts.

Real-world Applications: Connect mathematical concepts to real-life scenarios to enhance relevance and understanding.

Formative Assessments: Regularly check students' understanding during the learning process, making adjustments as necessary.

Incorporate Technology: Digital tools and apps can offer personalized practice and immediate feedback, catering to today's tech-savvy students.

Understanding Linguistic, Cultural, and Socioeconomic Diversity in the Math Classroom

Every classroom is a mosaic of diverse backgrounds, cultures, languages, and economic contexts. The modern educator must ensure that all students, regardless of their background, have equal opportunities to succeed. In the realm of mathematics, this means delivering instruction that acknowledges, respects, and leverages this diversity.

1. Linguistic Diversity:

Description: Recognizing that students come with different language backgrounds, proficiency levels, and dialects.

Implication for Teaching: Provide multi-modal instruction, integrating visuals, real-world examples, and hands-on activities. Use clear, concise language and consider incorporating math vocabulary in multiple languages.

2. Cultural Diversity:

Description: Understanding that students' cultural backgrounds influence their perspectives, values, and learning styles.

Implication for Teaching: Incorporate culturally relevant examples in math problems. Respect and celebrate different ways of understanding and solving problems.

3. Socioeconomic Diversity:

Description: Recognizing that students come from varied economic backgrounds, which can impact their access to resources, experiences, and even their perspective on certain problems.

Implication for Teaching: Ensure that all materials and resources are accessible to every student. Avoid examples or problems that might alienate students based on their economic background.

Strategies for Relating Math to Students' Lives and Communities:

Contextualized Problems: Design math problems around real-world situations familiar to the students' community or daily lives.

Local and Cultural References: Incorporate landmarks, events, or cultural practices from the students' community into lessons.

Collaborative Projects: Allow students to share their diverse methods and approaches to problem-solving, fostering mutual respect and understanding.

Invite Community Involvement: Host math-related community events or invite local figures to share how they use math in their professions.

Culturally Relevant Pedagogy: Adapt the curriculum to include perspectives and contributions from diverse cultures, ensuring every student sees themselves represented in the math world.

Developmentally Appropriate Instruction & Transitions in Mathematical Representations

Introduction:

One of the hallmarks of effective math instruction is ensuring that it is tailored to the developmental level of the students while also challenging them to transition from concrete to abstract thinking. Understanding this progression is pivotal for educators as it influences how math concepts are introduced, practiced, and mastered.

1. Understanding Developmental Appropriateness in Math:

Developmental appropriateness is the practice of teaching in a way that is suitable for the age, grade level, and individual needs of students. In math, this ensures that students are taught concepts they are mentally ready for, ensuring better comprehension and engagement.

2. Transitions in Mathematical Representations:

a) Concrete Representations:

This is the 'hands-on' phase. It involves the use of physical objects to represent mathematical ideas.
Example: When teaching addition, students can use physical counters or tokens to combine groups and observe the results.

b) Symbolic (or Pictorial) Representations:

Transition from tangible items to pictures or diagrams.
Example: Drawing pictures of apples instead of using actual apples to solve an addition problem.

c) Abstract Representations:

At this level, students use numbers and mathematical symbols to represent ideas.
Example: Solving $2 + 3 = 5$ without the need for physical objects or pictures.

3. Building on Students' Strengths and Addressing Needs:

Every student comes to the classroom with a unique set of mathematical strengths and areas needing improvement. Recognizing and tapping into these strengths can motivate students and make learning more meaningful.

Addressing their needs might require differentiated instruction, remedial exercises, or additional resources like manipulatives.

4. Strategies for Implementing Developmentally Appropriate Instruction:

Use Assessments: Conduct pre-assessments to understand where each student stands concerning a particular concept. This can guide how you introduce new topics.

Introduce with Concrete Examples: Whenever introducing a new topic, start with tangible, real-world examples that students can touch and manipulate.

Transition Gradually: Move from concrete to symbolic to abstract representations over time. Ensure students are comfortable at one stage before pushing them to the next.

Differentiate Instruction: Remember that not all students will move through these stages at the same pace. Some may need more time with concrete or symbolic representations before they're ready for abstract thinking.

Provide Feedback: Regular feedback helps students understand where they stand and what they need to work on. It can guide them through the transitions between different types of representations.

Summary:

Understanding the developmental needs of students and the transitions between different types of mathematical representations is key to effective math instruction. By tuning into where each student is and guiding them through the progression from concrete to abstract thinking, educators can ensure that students grasp foundational concepts that will serve them well in more advanced math courses.

In preparation for the exam, reflect on how you might apply these principles in a classroom setting and be prepared to analyze teaching scenarios to determine if they reflect developmentally appropriate practices.

Using Manipulatives and Technological Tools in Mathematics Instruction

Introduction:

In the modern classroom, both physical manipulatives and technological tools play a pivotal role in fostering an understanding of mathematical concepts. When utilized effectively, these resources can elevate instruction and offer students a richer, more interactive learning experience.

1. Understanding the Role of Manipulatives:

Manipulatives are physical objects that students can handle to explore and learn mathematical concepts. They allow abstract ideas to take on a tangible form.

Examples: Counters, base-ten blocks, fraction bars, geoboards, number lines, and algebra tiles.

Benefits:
- Facilitate a concrete understanding of abstract mathematical concepts.
- Encourage active engagement and exploration.
- Enable students to visualize mathematical relationships and procedures.
- Support differentiated instruction, catering to various learning styles.

2. The Advent of Technological Tools:

Technological tools range from basic calculators to advanced software and apps designed to explore complex mathematical concepts.

Examples: Graphing calculators, digital math games, geometry software like GeoGebra, interactive math platforms like Desmos, and virtual manipulatives.

Benefits:
- Offer dynamic visualizations of mathematical concepts.
- Allow for instant feedback, enabling students to learn from mistakes in real-time.
- Facilitate individualized learning paths and adaptive practices.
- Provide opportunities for simulating real-world scenarios to apply math concepts.

3. Appropriate Use of Manipulatives and Technology:

Purposeful Selection: Choose tools and manipulatives that directly support the learning objective. For instance, algebra tiles are beneficial for visualizing polynomial operations, while graphing calculators are apt for exploring functions.

Intentional Integration: Seamlessly incorporate manipulatives and technology into lessons. They should enhance, not overshadow, the mathematical concepts being taught.

Monitor and Assess: Ensure that students are using the tools effectively and not just playing without purpose. Periodic checks and discussions can ensure they're on the right track.

Facilitate Transitions: Help students move from concrete (manipulatives) to symbolic (using numbers and symbols) to abstract (mental math and conceptual understanding).

For instance, after using base-ten blocks to understand place value, students should practice with written numbers and eventually solve related problems without the blocks.

4. Potential Challenges and Considerations:

Over-reliance: While tools are beneficial, students should not become overly dependent on them. The aim is for students to internalize concepts and not always need external aids.

Accessibility: Ensure all students have equal access to technological tools, both in class and, if possible, at home.

Training: Both educators and students may require training to use specific technological tools effectively.

Summary:

The strategic use of manipulatives and technological tools in the math classroom can greatly enhance student understanding and engagement. For the exam, be prepared to analyze teaching scenarios that involve these tools, identify their appropriate use, and recognize potential pitfalls. Reflect on how these resources fit into the broader instructional landscape, and consider how they can be best leveraged to support student learning.

Creating an Engaging Mathematical Learning Environment

Introduction:

For students to effectively grasp and retain mathematical concepts, a conducive and engaging learning environment is essential. Such an environment not only fosters mathematical understanding but also cultivates a love for the subject. This guide covers the elements of creating a classroom atmosphere that motivates all learners and promotes active engagement.

1. Elements of an Engaging Mathematical Environment:

Motivational Atmosphere: Encourage a growth mindset where effort is applauded, and mistakes are viewed as learning opportunities.

Variety of Tasks: Offer tasks that range from procedural to conceptual and from individual work to group projects.

Student Autonomy: Provide opportunities for students to take ownership of their learning, select their strategies, and approach problems in ways that make sense to them.

Relevance: Integrate real-world problems and scenarios that make the math meaningful to students' lives.

2. Task Selection and Presentation:

Interesting Tasks: Use problems that are open-ended, have multiple solutions, or require higher-order thinking.

Challenging Tasks: Offer problems that push students slightly out of their comfort zones but are within their reach with effort.

Worthwhile Tasks: Ensure tasks are aligned with learning objectives and offer value in terms of enhancing understanding.

3. Diverse Instructional Strategies:

Individual Work: Useful for assessments, deep thinking, and personalized practice.

Small-group Settings: Encourage collaboration, discussion, and multiple perspectives. Tasks like math stations, peer tutoring, or jigsaw activities can be effective.

Large-group Settings: Great for discussions, brainstorming, and whole-class activities. Techniques such as "Number Talks" or class debates on specific strategies can be beneficial.

4. Actively Engaging Students:

Interactive Technology: Use platforms like Desmos, Kahoot, or interactive whiteboards to make lessons more dynamic.

Manipulatives: Physical or virtual objects can help students visualize and explore concepts.

Math Games: Offer fun, competitive ways to practice skills.

Student-led Discussions: Encourage students to explain their thinking, ask questions, and challenge each other's ideas.

5. Cultivating a Positive Classroom Culture:

Encourage Risk-taking: Create a safe environment where students are unafraid to attempt challenging problems and possibly make mistakes.

Celebrate Diversity: Acknowledge and integrate diverse ways of thinking and problem-solving into the classroom.

Feedback: Offer timely, constructive feedback that guides students towards improvement.

6. Assessing Engagement:

Observation: Regularly monitor students during tasks. Look for signs of engagement, such as focus, discussion, and persistence.

Reflection: Have students reflect on their engagement and understanding regularly.

Feedback: Encourage students to give feedback on tasks – what they found engaging, what they didn't, and why.

Summary:

Creating an engaging mathematical environment requires a blend of effective task selection, diverse instructional strategies, and a positive, inclusive classroom culture. For the exam, you should be prepared to identify strategies that promote engagement, evaluate the effectiveness of given classroom scenarios, and suggest improvements based on best practices. Remember, the goal is not just to teach math, but to instill a lasting appreciation and enthusiasm for the subject in every student.

Using Various Tools to Enhance Mathematical Understanding

Introduction:

The effective use of diverse tools in a math classroom can significantly enhance students' conceptual understanding. These tools provide tangible or visual representations of abstract concepts, making them more comprehensible. This guide aims to elaborate on the variety of tools available and how they can be utilized to bolster mathematical understanding for students.

1. Importance of Tools in Mathematics Instruction:

Concrete Representation: Tools offer a tangible or visual representation of abstract mathematical concepts, aiding in understanding.

Engagement: Manipulatives and tools can make learning more interactive and fun, increasing student engagement.

Diverse Learners: Different tools cater to different learning styles, ensuring that all students can grasp concepts.

2. Types of Tools and Their Uses:

Counters (e.g., counting bears, tokens):
- Purpose: Helps with basic counting, addition, subtraction, and creating visual representations.
- Application: Useful for early math learners to grasp foundational concepts.

Standard and Nonstandard Units of Measure:
- Purpose: Introduces students to the concept of measurement.
- Application: Measure objects using unconventional units (e.g., paperclips) before transitioning to standard units.

Rulers and Protractors:
- Purpose: Measure length and angles.
- Application: Useful in geometry lessons, constructing shapes, and understanding the properties of shapes.

Scales:
- Purpose: Understand weight and balance.
- Application: Compare the weight of different objects, learn about units of mass.

Stopwatches:

- Purpose: Measure time intervals.
- Application: Useful in lessons about time, speed, or experiments involving timing.

Measuring Containers:

- Purpose: Understand volume and capacity.
- Application: Fill different containers to compare volume, understand concepts like "half" or "quarter" filled.

Money:

- Purpose: Learn about the value, addition, subtraction, and real-life math applications.
- Application: Role-playing shopping scenarios, making change, and budgeting exercises.

Calculators:

- Purpose: Perform calculations, explore mathematical functions.
- Application: Useful for complex calculations, understanding patterns, and verifying manual calculations.

Software (e.g., GeoGebra, Desmos):

- Purpose: Explore complex mathematical concepts, visualize data.
- Application: Plot graphs, understand geometric transformations, and explore advanced mathematical concepts.

3. Effective Implementation of Tools:

Purposeful Selection: Choose tools that align with the lesson's objective and are developmentally appropriate.

Model Proper Use: Demonstrate to students how to use the tools effectively and safely.

Guided Practice: Before allowing independent use, guide students in using the tools, providing opportunities for hands-on learning.

Incorporate Real-life Contexts: Use real-life scenarios where possible, making the math more relevant and meaningful.

4. Assessing Tool Use:

Observation: Monitor students as they use the tools, noting any misconceptions or innovative strategies.

Discussion and Reflection: Encourage students to discuss their experiences with the tools and reflect on how the tools enhanced their understanding.

Summary:

The array of tools available for mathematics instruction is vast, and selecting the right one can make a significant difference in students' understanding. As you prepare for the exam, familiarize yourself with the various tools and their applications in the classroom. Understand the importance of choosing the right tool for the right concept and ensuring students use them effectively.

Implementing Instructional Methods in Mathematics

Introduction:

For mathematics instruction, it's vital to implement a variety of methods and tasks that not only align with these standards but also actively promote students' ability to understand and apply mathematical concepts.

2. Variety of Instructional Methods:

Direct Instruction: Teacher-led instruction that's explicit and structured. Useful for introducing new concepts.

Inquiry-Based Learning: Students explore mathematical concepts through questioning, problem-solving, and discovery.

Cooperative Learning: Students work in groups, promoting collaboration, discussion, and shared problem-solving.

Flipped Classroom: Students first explore topics at home through readings or videos, then engage in problem-solving and tasks in the classroom.

Differentiated Instruction: Tailoring instruction to meet individual needs. Grouping students based on readiness, interest, or learning profile.

3. Variety of Tasks Promoting Mathematical Abilities:

Problem-Solving Tasks: Situations where students use math processes to find solutions. Promotes critical thinking and application.

Real-world Applications: Contextual problems related to real-life scenarios. Helps in understanding the relevance of math.

Mathematical Investigations: In-depth exploration of a math concept or problem, encouraging deep understanding and persistence.

Games and Simulations: Engaging and interactive ways to reinforce and practice math skills.

Journaling: Writing about mathematical understanding, misconceptions, and processes.

4. Aligning Instruction with essential teaching principles:

Lesson Planning: Start by identifying the teaching objectives for the lesson. Ensure that instructional methods and tasks directly align with these objectives.

Assessments: Use both formative (ongoing) and summative (end of unit) assessments that measure mastery of teaching standards.

Continuous Reflection: Regularly review and adapt teaching methods based on student performance related to teaching objectives.

5. Supporting Diverse Learners:

Use of Manipulatives: Physical tools like counters, number lines, and geometric shapes can aid in conceptual understanding.

Technology Integration: Use apps, software, and online resources aligned with teaching principles to cater to diverse learning styles.

Scaffolded Instruction: Break down complex tasks or provide step-by-step guidance to help learners grasp challenging concepts.

6. Professional Development and Collaboration:

Stay updated with the latest in math education and teaching principles through professional development opportunities.

Collaborate with peers to share best practices, resources, and strategies for effective instruction.

Summary:

To excel in the exam, it's crucial to have a profound understanding of the principles for mathematics and the diverse instructional methods and tasks that support these standards. Emphasize alignment, adaptability, and the promotion of deep mathematical understanding and application in all teaching practices.

Developing Clear Learning Goals Based on the essential teaching principles in Mathematics

Introduction:

The foundation of effective teaching lies in clear and concise learning goals. By aligning these goals with the standards, educators can ensure a unified approach to mathematics education that meets state expectations.

1. Understanding the teaching principles:

Mathematics teaching principles Overview: These standards detail the knowledge and skills that students should master at every grade level.

Importance: They provide a roadmap for educators, ensuring uniformity and comprehensive coverage of key mathematical concepts across the state.

2. Developing Clear Learning Goals:

Definition: Learning goals are specific, measurable outcomes you want students to achieve by the end of a lesson or unit.

SMART Criteria: Goals should be Specific, Measurable, Achievable, Relevant, and Time-bound.

3. Planning Instruction:

Reverse Engineer the Lesson: Begin with the end in mind. Identify the desired learning outcomes and then plan instructional activities to achieve these outcomes.

Resources and Materials: Select textbooks, tools, and manipulatives that align with your learning goals.

Differentiation: Plan for diverse learners. Adjust instruction and provide resources to cater to varying student needs, ensuring every student can achieve the set learning goals.

4. Delivering Instruction:

Engaging Presentation: Use a mix of teaching methods – direct instruction, group work, hands-on activities, and technology integration – to keep students engaged.

Continuous Feedback: As you teach, provide feedback to students about their progress towards the learning goals. Adjust instruction as necessary.

5. Assessing and Reevaluating Instruction:

Formative Assessment: Use quizzes, class discussions, and interactive activities to gauge student understanding during instruction.

Summative Assessment: At the end of a unit or lesson, use tests, projects, or presentations to assess student mastery of the learning goals.

Alignment with essential teaching principles: Ensure that all assessments, both formative and summative, align with teaching standards.

Reevaluation: Based on assessment results, reevaluate and adjust your instruction. If many students didn't achieve a learning goal, revisit that topic with a different instructional strategy.

6. Professional Reflection and Growth:

Self-reflection: Regularly evaluate your teaching methods, effectiveness, and alignment. Adjust accordingly.

Collaboration: Share insights, challenges, and successes with colleagues. Collaborative discussions can provide new perspectives and strategies.

Professional Development: Attend workshops, seminars, and conferences that focus on effective instructional strategies in mathematics.

Summary:

Developing clear learning goals is a cyclic process of planning, delivering, assessing, and reevaluating instruction. Continuously align your goals with instructional standards, and be adaptable based on student needs and assessment results. Mastery of this process will position you well for success on the exam.

Connecting Mathematics to the Real World and Other Disciplines

Introduction:

One of the key aspects of effective math instruction is demonstrating the applicability and ubiquity of mathematical concepts in the real world and across various disciplines. This approach not only enhances understanding but also cultivates a genuine appreciation for mathematics.

1. The Importance of Making Connections:

Relevance and Context: By linking math concepts to real-world situations, students can see the practical application of what they're learning, which often leads to deeper understanding and retention.

Interdisciplinary Learning: Drawing connections between math and other subjects showcases the interconnectedness of knowledge, fostering a more holistic learning experience.

2. Mathematics in the Real World:

Personal Finance: Use topics like interest rates, budgeting, and savings to teach algebraic functions and percentages.

Architecture and Construction: Geometry and measurement come alive when discussing the design of buildings, bridges, and other structures.

Sports: Statistics, probability, and measurement can be introduced through the analysis of sports games, player statistics, and game strategies.

3. Mathematics and Art:

Symmetry and Patterns: Explore symmetry in nature and art, linking to geometrical transformations.

Golden Ratio: Discuss its presence in art, nature, and architecture, offering a tangible link to ratios and proportions.

4. Mathematics and Music:

Rhythm and Time Signatures: Relate to fractions and division.

Sound Frequencies: Connect to wave functions and algebra.

Patterns and Sequences: Many musical compositions follow mathematical patterns, which can be analyzed and predicted.

5. Mathematics and Science:

Physics: Kinematics (distance, speed, time calculations), wave functions, and force diagrams offer myriad mathematical applications.

Chemistry: Moles and molarity concepts link to ratios and algebraic functions.

Biology: Genetics (Punnett squares) connects with probability.

6. Mathematics and Social Science:

Population Studies: Exponential growth and decay functions, statistics in census data.

Economics: Supply and demand curves, market equilibrium, and cost functions are intrinsically mathematical.

7. Mathematics and Business:

Stock Market Analysis: Graphing and analyzing stock market trends using statistical tools.

Business Operations: Inventory management, profit and loss calculations, and market analysis are grounded in mathematical reasoning.

8. Strategies to Help Students Make Connections:

Real-World Problems: Frame mathematical problems within a real-world context. Instead of just a generic word problem, use scenarios students can relate to.

Interdisciplinary Projects: Collaborate with teachers from other subjects to develop projects that require students to use skills from multiple disciplines.

Field Trips: Visits to museums, businesses, or science centers can provide tangible examples of math in the real world.

Guest Speakers: Invite professionals from various fields to discuss how they use math in their careers.

9. Assessing Connections:

Reflections and Journals: Ask students to write about how they see math in the world around them or in their favorite hobbies.

Project-Based Assessments: Assess students' ability to apply math concepts in real-world or interdisciplinary projects.

Summary:

Linking mathematics to real-world applications and other academic disciplines enhances understanding, interest, and the perceived value of the subject. To excel in the exam, aspiring educators should be proficient in bridging these connections, ensuring their students recognize the universality and applicability of mathematical concepts.

Questioning Strategies in Mathematical Discourse

Introduction:

Promoting mathematical discourse is fundamental in ensuring that students not only acquire mathematical knowledge but also develop analytical skills to critique and understand their mathematical thinking. Questioning is a central technique in this endeavor, and its efficacy is influenced by the types and delivery of the questions posed.

1. Importance of Questioning in Mathematics:

Promote Higher Order Thinking: Encourages students to think beyond the basic solution, exploring why a solution works and its broader implications.

Facilitate Self-assessment: Enables students to reflect on and evaluate their own understanding and thinking processes.

Stimulate Discourse: Engages students in mathematical discussions, allowing them to learn from peers.

2. Types of Questions:

Open-ended Questions: These do not have a single correct answer and invite students to think critically and creatively. Example: "Can you think of another way to solve this problem?"

Probing Questions: Dive deeper into students' answers to understand their thought processes. Example: "Why did you choose that method?"

Reflective Questions: Encourage students to consider the broader implications, relations, or applications of a mathematical concept. Example: "How does this concept relate to what we learned last week?"

Clarifying Questions: Aid in understanding a student's perspective and correct misconceptions. Example: "Can you explain that step in more detail?"

3. Strategies to Encourage Mathematical Discourse:

Wait Time: After posing a question, give students a moment to think before answering. This increases the likelihood of thoughtful responses.

Think-Pair-Share: Students first think individually, then discuss with a partner, and finally share with the whole class.

Socratic Questioning: A method of systematic questioning to stimulate critical thinking and illuminate ideas.

4. Evaluating Student Responses:

Affirmation and Extension: Acknowledge correct answers, and then pose an additional question to deepen understanding.

Redirecting: If a student's answer is incorrect, instead of immediate correction, redirect the question to the class or rephrase it to guide the student to the correct answer.

5. Building a Safe Environment:

Ensure that the classroom is a safe space where students feel comfortable sharing their thoughts, making mistakes, and learning from them.

Establish classroom norms for discourse, emphasizing respect, active listening, and constructive feedback.

6. Addressing Common Barriers:

Fear of Speaking: Some students may be hesitant to share. Encourage participation by validating all contributions and emphasizing the learning process over the correctness of answers.

Dominant Speakers: Ensure that all voices are heard by occasionally directing questions towards quieter students or using techniques like "turn and talk" to ensure everyone has a chance to speak.

7. The Role of Technology:

Digital platforms like discussion boards or math-specific forums can be used to facilitate mathematical discourse outside of classroom hours.

Tools like digital whiteboards can help in visualizing and sharing mathematical concepts and solutions.

8. Assessing the Quality of Discourse:

Engagement: Are all students actively participating?

Depth: Are students critically analyzing and evaluating mathematical concepts?

Collaboration: Are students building on each other's ideas?

Summary:

Effective questioning is pivotal in cultivating an environment of active mathematical discourse. By mastering diverse questioning techniques and strategies, educators can guide students towards deeper understanding, critical thinking, and reflective learning in mathematics. To excel in the exam, it's essential to be well-versed in these techniques and their role in mathematical instruction.

Assessments and Scoring Procedures in Mathematical Understanding

Introduction:

Assessment is a pivotal component of the instructional process. By understanding both formal and informal assessment strategies, teachers can gauge student understanding, identify misconceptions, and discern patterns of errors. Implementing a combination of these methods allows for a holistic understanding of student progress and areas of improvement.

1. Importance of Assessments in Mathematics:

Diagnostic Tool: Determine prior knowledge and identify misconceptions.

Monitor Progress: Track student growth and development over time.

Guidance for Instruction: Assessments guide lesson planning, helping teachers determine pacing, depth, and remediation needs.

Feedback Mechanism: Provides students with insight into their understanding and areas of improvement.

2. Formal Assessments:

Definition: Structured evaluations that often result in a grade or score.

Types:
- **Summative Assessments**: Administered after instruction to measure student mastery, e.g., end-of-unit tests, midterms, finals.
- **Benchmark Assessments**: Periodic tests, often standardized, to gauge student performance against a set standard.
- **Performance Tasks**: Require students to apply their skills and knowledge in a demonstrative way, e.g., project-based tasks.

3. Informal Assessments:

Definition: Ongoing observations and reviews that are often not graded but offer insight into student understanding.

Types:
- **Observations**: Watching students as they work, noting behaviors and strategies.
- **Question & Answer Sessions**: Spontaneous class discussions or Q&A sessions.
- **Exit Tickets**: Quick post-lesson evaluations where students write down one thing they've learned.
- **Think-Pair-Share**: Allows students to think individually, discuss with a peer, and then share insights with the class.

4. Scoring Procedures:

Rubrics: Defined criteria for assessing a student's performance on essays, projects, or complex tasks.

Checklists: Lists of items or criteria to be checked off as they are identified or achieved.

Anecdotal Notes: Informal notes taken by the teacher during observations.
Self and Peer Assessments: Students assess their own or their peers' work.

5. Evaluating Mathematical Understanding:

Focus on processes as well as results. A correct answer with the wrong method or a wrong answer with a partially correct method can offer insights.

Look for patterns in errors to identify widespread misconceptions or areas that need reteaching.

6. Addressing Common Misconceptions and Error Patterns:

Misconceptions: Fundamental misunderstandings of concepts. For example, thinking multiplication always makes numbers larger.

Error Patterns: Repeated mistakes that follow a pattern, e.g., consistently misplacing the decimal in division problems.

7. Feedback and Adjustments:

Use assessment results to provide constructive feedback, highlighting both strengths and areas of improvement. Adjust instructional plans and strategies based on assessment findings. For persistent misconceptions, consider revisiting concepts using a different approach.

8. Ethical Considerations:

Ensure assessments are fair, unbiased, and appropriate for the age and developmental level of students.

Use multiple forms of assessment to get a comprehensive view of student understanding.

Summary:

Assessments, both formal and informal, are indispensable tools in a math teacher's arsenal. Not only do they provide a snapshot of student understanding at a given moment, but they also chart a roadmap for future instruction. By being adept in various assessment and scoring methods, educators can effectively diagnose, intervene, and elevate the mathematical proficiency of their students. Mastering these concepts will be pivotal in succeeding in the exam.

Relationship Between Assessment and Instruction in Mathematics

Introduction:

A comprehensive understanding of the intricate relationship between assessment and instruction is pivotal for a mathematics educator. This dynamic ensures the continuous improvement of student learning. Additionally, catering to diverse learners, such as English-language learners, requires unique insights into assessment-driven instruction.

1. The Symbiotic Relationship of Assessment and Instruction:

Feedback Loop: Assessment provides data on student understanding, guiding subsequent instruction. Instruction, in turn, dictates the focus of future assessments.

Continuous Improvement: This dynamic relationship allows for the refinement of teaching strategies based on student performance.

2. Types of Assessment:

Formative Assessments: Ongoing evaluations during the instructional process. These help teachers understand where students are and adapt instruction accordingly.

Summative Assessments: Evaluations at the end of an instructional period to measure student understanding against standards.

3. Evaluating Assessment Results:

Analysis: Review results to identify patterns, such as common errors or misconceptions.

Reflection: Consider the effectiveness of the teaching strategies used.

Adjustment: Modify teaching techniques based on assessment outcomes.

4. Designing and Modifying Instruction:

Diagnostic Instruction: Using initial assessments to understand students' current

knowledge and skills. Helps in tailoring instruction to fit individual needs.

Differentiated Instruction: Tailoring instruction to meet individual student needs. This could involve grouping students by skill levels, offering varying resources, or modifying content.

5. Addressing the Needs of English-language Learners (ELLs):

Language Proficiency: Consider the language proficiency of ELLs when interpreting assessment results. Misunderstandings might be rooted in language barriers rather than mathematical concepts.

Scaffolding: Use visual aids, gestures, and clear language to support understanding. Provide additional resources, like glossaries or bilingual dictionaries.

Cultural Considerations: Be aware of cultural differences that might affect the understanding or interpretation of mathematical concepts or questions.

6. Monitoring Progress:

Ongoing Assessment: Regularly check in on students' progress to ensure that modified instruction is effective.

Feedback: Offer consistent feedback to students. This allows them to understand their strengths and areas that need improvement.

7. Collaborative Efforts:

Peer Assessments: Encourage students to assess and learn from each other. This can provide additional insights into their understanding.

Parental Involvement: Engage with parents, especially of ELLs, to understand the student's background and optimize their learning experience.

8. Ethical Implications:

Ensure that assessments are unbiased and fair for all students.

Consider the unique challenges faced by ELLs and provide accommodations as necessary.

Summary:

Understanding the relationship between assessment and instruction is foundational in a math educator's toolkit. This ensures a responsive and adaptive teaching methodology that caters to the diverse needs of students, especially ELLs. Grasping these nuances will be essential for excelling in the exam.

Understanding the Purpose, Characteristics, and Uses of Assessments in Mathematics

Introduction:

Assessment in mathematics is a multifaceted tool designed to gauge students' knowledge, skills, and understanding of mathematical concepts. To effectively guide instruction and promote student learning, teachers must understand the different types of assessments, their purposes, and how best to employ them in the classroom.

1. Overview of Assessments in Mathematics:

Purpose: The primary goal of assessments is to gather information about students' mathematical knowledge, skills, and understanding. This information can guide instruction, provide feedback to students, and evaluate the effectiveness of instructional strategies.

2. Formative Assessments:

Definition: Assessments that take place during the learning process to inform instruction.

Purpose: To monitor student understanding and adjust teaching techniques in real-time.

Characteristics:
- **Immediate Feedback**: Provides quick insights into student understanding.
- **Flexible**: Can be informal (e.g., asking questions) or structured (e.g., quizzes).
- **Adaptive**: Informs ongoing instructional decisions.

Examples:
- Classroom discussions
- Observations
- Quizzes
- Homework assignments
- Journals
- Think-pair-share activities

3. Summative Assessments:

Definition: Assessments that evaluate student learning at the end of an instructional period.

Purpose: To judge the quality and quantity of student learning against a predetermined standard.

Characteristics:
- **Structured**: Typically more formal and standardized.
- **Performance Indicators**: Measures students' proficiency in specific content areas.
- **End-point**: Administered after instruction on a particular topic is completed.

Examples:
- End-of-unit tests
- Midterms and final exams
- Standardized tests
- Projects and presentations

4. Benefits of a Balanced Assessment System:

Comprehensive Understanding: Using both formative and summative assessments provides a complete picture of student understanding.

Immediate Action: Formative assessments allow for immediate action and adjustment of instructional strategies.

Long-term Planning: Summative assessments provide data that can guide long-term curriculum planning and development.

5. Effective Use of Assessments:

Align with Learning Goals: Ensure that assessments are aligned with the learning objectives for the unit or lesson.

Diverse Question Types: Utilize a mix of multiple-choice, short answer, and open-ended questions to gauge various aspects of student understanding.

Feedback: Always provide constructive feedback, helping students understand mistakes and areas of improvement.

6. Ethical Considerations:

Ensure that all assessments are fair, unbiased, and accessible to all students, including those with special needs or language barriers.
Use assessments for their intended purpose and avoid over-emphasizing high-stakes testing.

Summary:

A comprehensive understanding of the purpose, characteristics, and effective use of both formative and summative assessments is essential for math educators. These tools, when used correctly, enhance student learning, guide instruction, and help in the evaluation of teaching strategies. Mastery of these concepts will be crucial for success on the exam.

Integrating Mathematics in Careers, Professions, and the Workplace in Instruction

Introduction:

Mathematics is an integral part of many careers and professions. By understanding its applications in various fields, educators can deliver instruction that highlights the real-world relevance of mathematical concepts, thus making learning more engaging and meaningful for students.

1. Mathematics in Various Careers and Professions:

Science & Engineering: Mathematics is foundational. From modeling natural phenomena, analyzing data, to solving complex engineering problems, mathematics is crucial.

Economics & Finance: Quantitative analysis, predictions, budgeting, and other financial assessments all rely on mathematics.

Medicine: Biostatistics, dosage calculations, genetic research, and medical imaging all require mathematics.

Art & Design: Geometry, symmetry, scaling, and proportion are crucial in designing and creating art.

Information Technology: Coding, data analysis, and algorithm design are heavily reliant on mathematical principles.

2. Demonstrating Mathematics in the Workplace:

Real-world Problems: Use problems that professionals face in their jobs. For example, how architects use geometry in their designs or how financial analysts use algebra and statistics to make investment recommendations.

Guest Speakers: Invite professionals from various fields to discuss how they use mathematics in their roles.

Field Trips: Organize visits to workplaces, like construction sites or banks, to see mathematics in action.

3. Planning Effective Instruction:

Relevance: Always begin by explaining the relevance of the mathematical concept being taught. How is it used in the real world? Why might the student need it in a future career?

Practical Applications: When teaching a concept, provide practical examples. For instance, if teaching percentages, explain how it's used in calculating discounts, interest rates, and tax.

Projects: Assign projects that simulate real-world problems. For example, students can be given a budget and asked to plan a trip, incorporating various costs and using mathematics to stay within the budget.

4. Benefits of Integrating Career-Relevance in Math Instruction:

Engagement: Students are more engaged when they see the real-world relevance of what they're learning.

Retention: Real-world applications help students retain and recall information better.

Preparedness: Understanding the practical applications of mathematics prepares students for future careers and daily life tasks.

5. Challenges & Solutions:

Varied Interests: Not all students have the same career aspirations. It's crucial to provide a variety of examples to cater to diverse interests.

Complexity: Some real-world applications might be too complex for younger students. It's essential to simplify these applications or choose age-appropriate examples.

Summary:

Understanding the significance of mathematics in various careers and the workplace is vital for educators. By integrating this understanding into instruction, teachers can make mathematical concepts more engaging and relevant for students. Preparing for this aspect of the exam involves recognizing the importance of real-world applications and being able to integrate them effectively into lesson planning.

Number Concepts and Operations

Introduction

The foundation of mathematics is built on numbers, their properties, and the operations we perform with them. For educators aiming to excel in teaching mathematics, a deep understanding of these foundational elements is imperative.

As a test taker, this competency is an assessment of your grasp on essential number concepts, the intricacies of operations like addition, subtraction, multiplication, and division, and the properties associated with numbers and these operations. Mastery in this area is a reflection of your readiness to effectively teach and guide students through the foundational stages of their mathematical journey. By preparing for and excelling in this competency, you demonstrate your commitment to fostering a strong mathematical base in your students, enabling them to build upon these concepts with confidence as they progress in their academic endeavors.

Video lesson:
https://www.youtube.com/embed/Fc_E89nZLbw?si=gizwtVNTOW_njTwp

Video lesson:
https://www.youtube.com/embed/hzkUPBx4ptE?si=KHUI3fvT1Yh6jeMr

1. Understand Key Terms and Concepts:

Integers: Whole numbers (both positive and negative) and zero.

Positive Integers:

1, 2, 3, 4, 5, 6, 7, 8, 9, 10, ... and so on.

Negative Integers:

-1, -2, -3, -4, -5, -6, -7, -8, -9, -10, ... and so on.

Zero:

0

Integers are like whole numbers, but they also include negative numbers. Remember, fractions are not integers!

Integers can also be **negative** {−1, −2,−3, −4, ... }, **positive** {1, 2, 3, 4, ... }, or **zero** {0}

We can put all of this together:

Integers = { ..., −4, −3, −2, −1, 0, 1, 2, 3, 4, ... }

Examples: −15, −2, 0, 3 and 197 are all integers.

(But numbers like ½, 1.6 and 3.9 are not integers)

Rational Numbers: Numbers that can be written as a fraction (quotient) of two integers. To better understand the meaning of a rational number, look at the root word - **ratio** (a fraction). If a number has a ratio, it is a *rational* number. Let's look at this further:

Example: 0.5 is rational, because it can be written as the ratio 1/2

Example: 8 is rational, because it can be written as the ratio 8/1

Example 0.666 is rational, because it can be written as the ratio 2/3

Irrational Numbers: Numbers that can't be written as a ratio (fraction)

Example: π (Pi) is an irrational number. We cannot write a fraction that represents the long 3.14… number that is made up of Pi, even though we know that 22/7 is a close approximation, the decimal begins to trail away from the actual number of Pi.

Therefore, the test whether or not a number is rational or irrational depends on if we can write the number as a simple fraction.

Example: 8.5 can be written as a simple fraction like 17/2.

So 8.5 is a rational number, and therefore not an irrational number.

Here are some more examples:

Number	Fraction	Rational or Irrational?
4.75	19/4	Rational
0.004	1/250	Rational
√2	√2	Irrational

Real Numbers: All numbers that can be plotted on a number line, including both rational and irrational numbers.

Real Numbers include: 2, 3.48, −0.7431, ⅚, π (pi), 1,985,673

Pretty much every number you can think of is a Real Number.

To confirm real numbers include:
- Whole Numbers (like 0, 1, 2, 3, 4, etc)
- Rational Numbers (like 2/3, 0.5, 0.666..., 1.8, etc)
- Irrational Numbers (like π, √2, etc)

Real Numbers include positive and negative numbers as well as zero.

So the question is: What's NOT a Real Number?
- Imaginary Numbers like $\sqrt{-1}$ (the square root of minus 1) are not Real Numbers
- Infinity is not a Real Number

Video lesson:
https://www.youtube.com/embed/3ydlNhTBrhY?si=s5SsFS1TD4xlb8Dw

Video lesson:
https://www.youtube.com/embed/VHjC7Fk0ZJM?si=6KJhGjxUQBilZZKt

Video lesson:
https://www.youtube.com/embed/As2FNVz9qG4?si=ZLVnpP6O4rypwiNU

I. Basic operations with integers:

Addition: $-3 + 2 = -1$

Subtraction: $5 - 7 = -2$

Multiplication: $-4 \times 6 = -24$

Division (Note: Division by zero is undefined): $8 \div -4 = -2$

II. Operations with rational numbers:

Addition: $1 / 2 + 1 / 3 = 5 / 6$

Subtraction: $2 / 3 - 1 / 2 = 1 / 6$

Multiplication: $1 / 4 \times 2 / 3 = 2 / 12 = 1 / 6$

Division: $3 / 4 \div 2 / 3 = 9 / 8$

2. Familiarize with Number Properties:

Commutative Property: The order of numbers does not affect the result (applies to both addition and multiplication).

Associative Property: The grouping of numbers does not affect the result (also applies to both addition and multiplication).

Distributive Property: Expanding multiplication over addition or subtraction.

Identity Property: The sum of any number and zero is the number itself (for addition) and the product of any number and one is the number itself (for multiplication).

Inverse Property: Every number has an inverse such that their sum (for addition) or product (for multiplication) will yield the identity number.

Adding or Multiplying Odd and Even Numbers

What are the consistent patterns when you add or multiply odd and even numbers? Here are some established truths when dealing with the addition or multiplication of odd and even figures:

Addition:
- The sum of two odd numbers is even.
- The sum of two even numbers is even.
- The sum of an odd and an even number is odd.

Multiplication:
- The product of two odd numbers is odd.
- The product of two even numbers is even.
- The product of an odd and an even number is even.

Video lesson:
https://www.youtube.com/embed/us1OhnJXZQY?si=SoKk TruNpXKQcsxh

Video lesson:
https://www.youtube.com/embed/89-5jU9A1Q4?si=Vtzg3w da35tPbhe2

Understanding Equivalency in Mathematics:

1. Different Representations of Rational Numbers

A rational number can be represented in various forms such as a fraction, a decimal, or a percent. Let's take the number 3/4 as an example:

- **Fraction**: 3/4
- **Decimal**: 0.75
- **Percent**: 75%

All three of these are equivalent representations of the same value.

2. Equivalency between Fractions

Fractions can be equivalent even if their numerators and denominators are different. For example: 1/2 is equivalent to 2/4, 3/6, 4/8, and so on.

3. Equivalency in Mathematical Expressions

Let's understand this with the distributive property. Consider:

$a(b + c) = ab + ac$

This means, if you distribute variable a across the parentheses, the resulting expression is equivalent to the original one.

4. Simplification

Another way to demonstrate understanding is by simplifying expressions. For example: $6x^2y/3xy$ can be simplified to $2x$. Both expressions are equivalent, just presented differently.

5. Decimal and Fraction Equivalency

Consider the decimal 0.333... This is equivalent to the fraction 1/3. Another example is 0.6 which is equivalent to 3/5.

In case it's been a while, here are the steps to do that:

1. Write 0.6 as 0.6/1
2. Multiply the numerator and the denominator by 10 for each digit after the decimal point.
3. 0.6 x 10 = 6; and 1 x 10 = 6. Now we have 6/10
4. Now, I can see that both 6 and 10 are even, so this fraction can be reduced. To reduce the fraction, we need to find the Greatest Common Factor (GCF) for 6 and 10. Remember that a factor is simply a number that divides into another number without any remainder let over.
5. Now, we must list out the factors:
   a. The factors of 6 are: 1, 2, 3, 6
   b. The factors of 10 are: 1, 2, 5, 10
      i. The GCF for both 6 and 10 is: 2
6. This means that 2 is the largest number that we can reduce both 6 and 10 by. In this next step, we divide 6/2 = 3, and 10/2 = 5
7. And there we have our answer ⅗!

6. Converting Between Forms

It's important to be able to switch between forms efficiently. For example:
- **To convert a fraction to a decimal**: Divide the numerator by the denominator.
  - **Example**: ¾ → 3 ÷ 4 = 0.75 → 0.75

- **To convert a decimal to a fraction**: Write the decimal over its place value (like 10, 100, 1000, etc.) and simplify if needed.
  - **Example**: 0.8 → Write 0.8 as 8/10, then simplify. → 4/5

- **To convert a decimal to a percent**: Multiply the decimal by 100.
  - **Example**: 0.45 → 0.45 × 100 = 45% → 45%

- **To convert a percent to a decimal**: Divide the percent by 100.
  - **Example**: 90% → 90 ÷ 100 = 0.9 → 0.9

By recognizing these equivalencies, you will be better equipped to solve math problems on your exam in smart, flexible ways!

Video lesson:
https://www.youtube.com/embed/W2vufcayZnA?si=rQTfTnbO94WR5deo

Video lesson:
https://www.youtube.com/embed/Qfcra7xQnR4?si=WoT_igomi8jFEENv

Video lesson:
https://www.youtube.com/embed/hSB_HAZfZFo?si=cOWCF5wmBhJGtn0q

Factors

Factors are whole numbers that, when multiplied together, give another specific number without leaving any remainder.

Here is a list of common divisibility rules:

Divisible by	If:
2	Last digit is 0, 2, 4, 6, or 8
3	Sum of digits is divisible by 3
4	Last 2 digits are divisible by 4
5	Last digit is 0 or 5
6	Number is divisible by 2 or 3
8	Last 3 digits are divisible by 8
9	Sum of digits is divisible by 9
10	Last digit is 0

Factoring

Factoring a number involves identifying all the whole numbers that can multiply to give that number. Generally, these factors are arranged in ascending order.

A practical approach to find the factors of a number is to begin with the number 1 and continue pairing it up with other numbers. The process can be stopped once you find a number that has already been identified in a previous pairing.

For instance, when determining the factors of 16:

1 and 16,

2 and 8,

4 and 4.

So, the factors of 16 are 1, 2, 4, 8, and 16.

Prime Factorization

Prime numbers are unique numbers greater than 1 that are divisible only by 1 and themselves. For instance, 23 is a prime number because only 1 and 23 divide it evenly.

Some prime numbers include:

2, 3, 5, 7, 11, 13, 19, 37, 41, and 43.

Prime factorization is the process of breaking down a number into its prime components. It's especially useful in determining the highest common factor or the lowest common multiple among numbers, but there are multiple methods to achieve those.

To demonstrate, let's break down the number 42:

42 can be divided into the factors 2 and 21. Here, 2 is a prime, but 21 isn't. Further dividing 21, we get the factors 3 and 7 - both of which are prime.

Using a factor tree:

From 42, we have branches to 2 and 21. From 21, it further branches out to 3 and 7. All terminal points, 2, 3, and 7 are prime numbers.

Thus, the prime factorization of 42 is 2 x 3 x 7.

Greatest Common Factor

The greatest common factor (GCF) is the highest number by which two numbers can be evenly divided. To determine the GCF, you can either:

1. Identify all factors of each number and pick the largest one they share.
2. Decompose each number into its prime factors and then multiply the common prime factors.

An event manager has 50 chairs, 75 tables, and 100 banners. She wants to create booths using all these items, ensuring that each booth has an equal number of chairs, tables, and banners. What's the greatest number of booths she can set up?

Factors of 50: 1, 2, 5, 10, 25, 50
Factors of 75: 1, 3, 5, 15, 25, 75
Factors of 100: 1, 2, 4, 5, 10, 20, 25, 50, 100

From the above, the largest common factor is 25.

Alternatively, through prime factorization:
50 = 2 x 5 x 5
75 = 3 x 5 x 5
100 = 2 x 2 x 5 x 5

By multiplying the common prime numbers: 5 x 5 = 25.

This suggests that the event manager can arrange a maximum of 25 booths. Each booth will be equipped with 2 chairs (50/25), 3 tables (75/25), and 4 banners (100/25).

Multiples

Multiples are the product of a specific number and any given whole number. To determine the initial multiples of a particular number, simply start multiplying it by integers beginning from 1.

For instance, when seeking the early multiples of 3, you can multiply it by integers starting at 1:

- 3×1=3
- 3×2=6
- 3×3=9
- 3×4=12

Least Common Multiple

The smallest number that two numbers can both divide into without leaving a remainder is called their least common multiple. There are a couple of methods to determine this:

- List the multiples of each number until a mutual multiple is spotted.
- Find the prime factorization of both numbers, and then multiply all distinct factors.

For instance, consider the situation where pencils are sold in packs of 7 and erasers in packs of 5. If Lucy wants to purchase an equal number of pencils and erasers, how many of each should she buy?

To determine this, let's look at the initial multiples for both:

5: 5, 10, 15, 20, 25, 30, 35, ...

7: 7, 14, 21, 28, 35, 42, ...

The smallest mutual multiple for 5 and 7 is 35.

Alternatively, using prime factorization:

5 is a prime number on its own.

7 is also prime.

Thus, the least common multiple for 5 and 7 is 5 × 7 = 35
5×7=35.

To have an equal number of pencils and erasers, Lucy should buy items in sets of 35. This means she'd need 5 packs of pencils and 7 packs of erasers to achieve this.

Understanding Equivalency of Rational Numbers and Mathematical Expressions

Rational numbers are any numbers that can be expressed as the quotient or fraction p/q of two integers, where p is the numerator and q is the nonzero denominator. A strong understanding of equivalency among different representations is crucial, as it allows for flexibility in mathematical computations and a deeper comprehension of the nature of numbers.

1. Different Representations of Rational Numbers:

Rational numbers can be represented in various ways:

Fractions: 2/3

Decimals: 0.666...

Percents: 66.66...

These different representations can describe the same value. For instance, 1/2 is equivalent to 0.5 or 50%.

2. Converting Between Representations:

Fraction to Decimal: Divide the numerator by the denominator.
3/4 is equivalent to 0.75 when you divide 3 by 4.

Decimal to Percent: Multiply the decimal by 100.

0.75 as a percentage is 75%.

Percent to Fraction: Write the percent as a fraction over 100 and then simplify.

75% is equivalent to 75/100 or 3/4 upon simplification.

3. Equivalency between Mathematical Expressions:

Two mathematical expressions are equivalent if they represent the same value. For example:

3 + 2 is equivalent to 4 + 1

2x + 3x is equivalent to 5x

Understanding equivalency can also involve:

Factoring: Expressing an algebraic expression as the product of its factors.

$x^2 - 9$ is equivalent to $(x + 3)(x - 3)$

Expanding: Multiplying out to express the expression in a more extended form.

$(x + 3)(x - 3)$ is equivalent to $x^2 - 9$

Simplifying: Combining like terms or reducing the expression to its simplest form.

4x + 2x simplifies to 6x

4. Properties to Understand Equivalency:

Commutative Property: The order of addition or multiplication doesn't affect the result.

$a + b = b + a$

$ab = ba$

Associative Property: The grouping in addition or multiplication doesn't affect the result.

$(a + b) + c = a + (b + c)$

$(ab)c = a(bc)$

Distributive Property: Helps in expanding or factoring expressions.

$a(b + c) = ab + ac$

5. Examples and Practice:

Converting Between Representations:

- Express 0.45 as a fraction.
- Convert 7/20 to a percentage.

Identifying Equivalency:

- Are $3x + 4y$ and $4y + 3x$ equivalent?
- Is $x^2 + 2x + 1$ equivalent to $(x + 1)(x + 1)$?

Final Notes:

Understanding the equivalency among different representations of rational numbers and between mathematical expressions is fundamental. This knowledge ensures you can fluently transition between various mathematical forms to simplify calculations or to better understand the underlying relationships in a problem. Practice is key! The more problems you solve, the more comfortable you'll be with recognizing equivalencies.

Video lesson:
https://www.youtube.com/embed/c_Ep1zIncic?si=HQcOp M58d0qDL-Ad

Video lesson:
https://www.youtube.com/embed/cyE2rTvFuso?si=zNAZVi nB-bw9KNke

Video lesson:
https://www.youtube.com/embed/x0AGYMQqFyk?si=qbMx
ZcNi0Yg43-Os

Representations of Real Numbers

Introduction to Real Numbers

Definition: Real numbers encompass both rational and irrational numbers. Rational numbers can be expressed as a fraction (e.g., 2/3, 7, -5), while irrational numbers can't be precisely expressed as a fraction (e.g., $\sqrt{2}$, π).

Different Representations of Real Numbers

Fractions: A/B where A and B are integers, and B is not zero.

Decimals: Numbers expressed in the base-10 system.
Can be terminating (e.g., 0.75) or repeating (e.g., 0.333...).

Percents: A way to express a number as a fraction of 100.

Situational Selection of Representations

Fractions:

- When to use: Situations involving part-to-whole relationships, or when the emphasis is on ratios.
- Example: If 4 out of 5 dentists recommend a toothpaste, this can be represented as 4/5.

Decimals:

- **When to use**: Useful in everyday calculations, money, measurements, or when precision is required.
- **Example**: When discussing the distance traveled, you might say 0.75 miles.

Percents:

- **When to use**: Comparison, financial situations, growth/shrinkage rates, or when discussing proportions relative to a whole.
- **Example**: Sales tax, discounts, or when saying "60% of students passed the exam."

Conversion between Representations

Fraction to Decimal: Divide the numerator by the denominator.

- 3/4 becomes 0.75
- Decimal to Percent: Multiply by 100.
- 0.75 becomes 75%

Percent to Fraction: Divide by 100 and simplify.

- 75% becomes 75/100 which simplifies to 3/4

Practice with Real-Life Situations

Situation: You bake a pie and eat 1/8 of it. What decimal represents the portion eaten?

Situation: A product has a 20% discount. What fraction of the original price will you save?

Situation: Your bank's interest rate is 0.05. What percentage is this?

Tips for the Exam

Always think about the context: The choice between fraction, decimal, or percent often hinges on the specific scenario.

Comparative Language:

Greater Than (>): A number is to the right on the number line compared to another number.

Less Than (<): A number is to the left on the number line compared to another number.

Equal (=): Two numbers occupy the same point on the number line.

Greater Than or Equal To ($\geq$): A number is to the right or at the same point on the number line.

Less Than or Equal To ($\leq$): A number is to the left or at the same point on the number line.

Sets of Objects for Representation:

Number Lines: Useful for visualizing the order and relative magnitude of numbers.

Whole Numbers: Start at 0 and go to the right.

Integers: Include both positive and negative numbers.

Rational Numbers: Placed according to their decimal or fraction value.

Real Numbers: All numbers on the number line, including points for irrational numbers.

Dot Plots: Useful for visualizing frequency or distribution of numbers.

Bar Graphs: Useful for comparing the magnitude of different categories.

Pie Charts: Can represent fractions or percentages of a whole.

Video lesson:
https://www.youtube.com/embed/g8eez2nkGo0?si=vYboL
CxX2SP-iFdM

Using Of A Variety Of Models And Objects For Representing Numbers

1. Number Lines:

Definition: A straight line on which every point corresponds to a number.
Usage: Helps visualize order and spacing of numbers.
Can represent whole numbers, integers, rational numbers, and irrational numbers.
Especially useful for understanding negative numbers, fractions, and the concept of distance between numbers.

2. Fraction Strips:

Definition: Bars or strips divided into equal parts to represent fractions.

Usage: Compare the size of different fractions.
Understand equivalent fractions (e.g., ½ is the same size as 2/4 on a fraction strip).
Visualize operations with fractions, like adding ⅓ + ¼.

3. Diagrams:

Definition: Pictorial representations of numbers or mathematical situations.

Usage: Pie charts can visually represent parts of a whole (like fractions or percentages).

Venn diagrams can represent set theory concepts and relationships.

4. Patterns:

Definition: Recognizable and repeatable designs or sequences.

Usage: Understand sequences in numbers, such as arithmetic or geometric sequences.
Predict future numbers or elements in a sequence.
Recognize growth patterns, such as in multiplication tables.

5. Shaded Regions:

Definition: Parts of a figure or area colored differently to represent a portion or fraction of the whole.

Usage: Grids with shaded cells can represent fractions or percentages.
Shapes like rectangles or circles with a shaded portion can represent parts of a whole.

6. Objects:

Definition: Concrete items or manipulatives used to represent numbers.

Usage: Counters or beads can represent whole numbers.
Base-10 blocks can be used to understand place value.
Algebra tiles can visually represent algebraic expressions.

Concrete And Visual Representations To Demonstrate The Connections Between Operations And Algorithms

1. Concrete Representations:

Definition: Physical items or manipulatives used to demonstrate math concepts.
Examples & Usage:

- **Base-10 Blocks**: Used for place value understanding, addition, subtraction, multiplication, and division. Can visually show carrying/borrowing in addition/subtraction.
- **Algebra Tiles**: Used for representing variables and constants. Facilitates understanding of algebraic operations, like combining like terms and solving equations.
- **Counters or Beads**: Helps in basic counting, addition, and subtraction. Introduces the concept of one-to-one correspondence.
- **Cuisenaire Rods**: Visualize fractions, ratios, and proportions.

2. Visual Representations:

Definition: Diagrams, models, charts, and drawings that demonstrate math concepts without necessarily being tangible items.
Examples & Usage:

Number Lines: Illustrate addition and subtraction (movement along the line). Shows multiplication as repeated addition. Conveys absolute value as distance from zero.

Area Models: Break down multiplication problems into sections. Can be used for polynomial multiplication in algebra.

Bar Models: Useful in understanding ratios, fractions, and percentages Helps solve word problems by visually representing known and unknown quantities.

Flowcharts: Demonstrate steps in algorithms or processes. Useful for visualizing sequences in problem-solving.

Grids: Use in coordinate geometry to plot points, lines, and shapes. Helps in visualizing transformations and reflections.

Connections Between Operations and Algorithms:

Operational Understanding: Concrete and visual tools make abstract operations tangible. For instance, using base-10 blocks helps understand why we carry over in addition.

Algorithm Visualization: When learning a new algorithm, visual aids can demystify the steps involved. Area models, for example, break down the multiplication process.

Conceptual Reinforcement: Visual and concrete tools help reinforce why algorithms work, not just how to do them. This deeper understanding is crucial for problem-solving and application.

Place value, rounding and other number properties

Introduction:

Understanding the concept of place value, rounding, and number properties is foundational for mathematics education. It allows us to easily perform mental calculations, make accurate estimations, and develop an intuitive understanding of numbers. This section will guide you through these concepts and provide examples to ensure you're well-prepared for this section of your test.

1. Place Value:

Place value refers to the position of a number and its corresponding value.

Example:

In the number 7,482:

7 is in the thousands place

4 is in the hundreds place

8 is in the tens place

2 is in the ones place

Key Concepts:
- A number in one place has ten times the value of the number in the place to its immediate right.
- Composing numbers means putting together smaller units to form larger numbers.
- Decomposing numbers means breaking down numbers into smaller units.

Practice:

Decompose the number 7,482.

Answer: 7,000 + 400 + 80 + 2

Compose a number using the following place values: 3 thousands, 5 hundreds, 4 tens, and 7 ones.

Answer: 3,547

Video lesson:
https://www.youtube.com/embed/sTBh8WvdW_w?si=pil9S
KcYb_avkzz6

2. Rounding:

Rounding is the process of approximating a number to its nearest specified value.

Key Concepts:
- When rounding to a particular place value, consider the digit immediately to the right.
- If that digit is 5 or greater, the number in the specified place value rounds up.
- If that digit is less than 5, the number in the specified place value stays the same.

Practice:
Round 7,482 to the nearest hundred.
Answer: 7,500

Round 3,547 to the nearest thousand.
Answer: 4,000

3. Number Properties:

Here are some key properties that are relevant:

a. **Commutative Property**: Changing the order of numbers doesn't change their sum or product.
Example: 3 + 7 = 7 + 3

b. **Associative Property**: Grouping of numbers doesn't change their sum or product.
Example: (3 + 5) + 7 = 3 + (5 + 7)

c. **Identity Property**: Adding 0 to a number doesn't change its value; multiplying a number by 1 doesn't change its value.

Example: 7 + 0 = 7 and 7 x 1 = 7

d. **Distributive Property**: Multiplying a sum by a number gives the same result as multiplying each addend separately and then adding the products.

Example: 3 x (4 + 2) = 3 x 4 + 3 x 2

4. Mental Mathematics and Computational Estimation:

Key Concepts:
- Estimating can help quickly determine approximate answers.
- Using benchmark numbers like 5, 10, 50, or 100 can assist in making estimations.

Practice:

Estimate the sum: 7,492 + 6,518.

Answer: 7,500 + 6,500 = 14,000

Estimate the product: 45 x 24.

Answer: 45 x 25 = 1,125 (used the benchmark number 25)

Video lesson:
https://www.youtube.com/embed/rmaNAKhxY_U?si=SAA EBOp4YaNSIlKf

Video lesson:
https://www.youtube.com/embed/MLbNhjghXJU?si=hFIf-g yy1s2qeopq

Video lesson:
https://www.youtube.com/embed/Jt7RumilkkA?si=uAu81G
kK4pw_bDXe

Fractions and operations

Introduction:

Fractions are fundamental in math education and daily life. Future educators should have a deep understanding of fractions, their representations, and the operations involving them. This section will walk you through the core concepts and provide practice examples to aid your preparation for the

test.

1. Fundamental Understanding of Fractions:

A fraction represents a part of a whole. It has a **numerator** (the top number) indicating the part being considered and a **denominator** (the bottom number) showing the number of equal parts the whole is divided into.

Example: In the fraction 3/4, 3 is the numerator and 4 is the denominator. This means we are considering 3 out of 4 equal parts.

2. Representations of Fractions:

Fractions can be represented in various ways, including:

a. **Pictorial Representation**: Using images, such as shaded parts of circles or rectangles.

b. **Number Line Representation**: Placing fractions on a number line between 0 and 1 or beyond.

c. **Decimal and Percentage Representation**: Converting fractions to decimals or percentages.

3. Operations Involving Fractions:

a. **Addition and Subtraction**: To add or subtract fractions, the denominators must be the same.
Example:
3/5 + 2/5 = 5/5 = 1

b. **Multiplication**: Multiply the numerators together and the denominators together.
Example:
3/5 x 2/3 = 6/15 = 2/5

c. **Division**: Multiply the first fraction by the reciprocal of the second fraction.
Example:
3/5 ÷ 2/3 = 3/5 x 3/2 = 9/10

d. **Simplification**: Reduce the fraction to its lowest terms.
Example:
6/8 = 3/4 (divided both the numerator and the denominator by their greatest common divisor, which is 2)

4. Teaching Fractions:

It's essential to use various approaches:
a. **Concrete Materials**: Use real-world objects like pizza slices or chocolates to introduce fractions.

b. **Fraction Manipulatives**: Tools like fraction strips or fraction circles can be beneficial.

c. **Real-world Situations**: Pose problems involving situations students encounter daily, like splitting a candy bar or sharing a jug of water.

d. **Technology Integration**: Use software or applications that offer interactive fraction exercises.

Integers, Rational Numbers and Real Numbers

1. Understand Key Terms and Concepts:

Integers: Whole numbers (both positive and negative) and zero.
Positive Integers:
1, 2, 3, 4, 5, 6, 7, 8, 9, 10, ... and so on.

Negative Integers:
-1, -2, -3, -4, -5, -6, -7, -8, -9, -10, ... and so on.

Zero:
0

Integers are like whole numbers, but they also include negative numbers. Remember, fractions are not integers!

Integers can also be **negative** $\{-1, -2, -3, -4, ... \}$, **positive** $\{1, 2, 3, 4, ... \}$, or **zero** $\{0\}$

We can put all of this together:
Integers = $\{ ..., -4, -3, -2, -1, 0, 1, 2, 3, 4, ... \}$

Examples: $-15, -2, 0, 3$ and 197 are all integers.
(But numbers like ½, 1.6 and 3.9 are not integers)

Rational Numbers: Numbers that can be written as a fraction (quotient) of two integers. To better understand the meaning of a rational number, look at the root word - **ratio** (a fraction). If a number has a ratio, it is a *rational* number. Let's look at this further:

Example: 0.5 is rational, because it can be written as the ratio 1/2

Example: 8 is rational, because it can be written as the ratio 8/1

Example 0.666 is rational, because it can be written as the ratio 1/6

Irrational Numbers: Numbers that can't be written as a ratio (fraction)

Example: π (Pi) is an irrational number. We cannot write a fraction that represents the long 3.14… number that is made up of Pi, even though we know that 22/7 is a close approximation, the decimal begins to trail away from the actual number of Pi.

Therefore, the test whether or not a number is rational or irrational depends on if we can write the number as a simple fraction.

Example: 8.5 can be written as a simple fraction like 17/2.

So 8.5 is a rational number, and therefore not an irrational number.

Here are some more examples:

Number	Fraction	Rational or Irrational?
4.75	19/4	Rational
0.004	1/250	Rational
√2	√2	Irrational

Real Numbers: All numbers that can be plotted on a number line, including both rational and irrational numbers.

Real Numbers include: 2, 3.48, −0.7431, ⅝, π (pi), 1,985,673

Pretty much every number you can think of is a Real Number.

To confirm real numbers include:

- Whole Numbers (like 0, 1, 2, 3, 4, etc)
- Rational Numbers (like 2/3, 0.5, 0.666..., 1.8, etc)
- Irrational Numbers (like π, √2, etc)

Real Numbers include positive and negative numbers as well as zero.

So the question is: What's NOT a Real Number?

- Imaginary Numbers like $\sqrt{-1}$ (the square root of minus 1) are not Real Numbers
- Infinity is not a Real Number

I. Basic operations with integers:

Definition: Integers include all whole numbers and their negative counterparts.

Example: ...,-3, -2, -1, 0, 1, 2, 3,...

Operations:

Addition: $-3 + 2 = -1$

Subtraction: $5 - 7 = -2$

Multiplication: $-4 \times 6 = -24$

Division (Note: Division by zero is undefined): $8 \div -4 = -2$

II. Operations with rational numbers:

Definition: Rational numbers are numbers that can be expressed as the quotient or

fraction p/q of two integers, a numerator p and a non-zero denominator q.

Example: 1/2, -3/4, 7, -5 (because they can be expressed as 7 / 1 , − 5 / 1)

Operations:

Addition: 1 / 2 + 1 / 3 = 5 / 6

Subtraction: 2 / 3 − 1 / 2 = 1 / 6

Multiplication: 1 / 4 × 2 / 3 = 2 / 12 = 1 / 6

Division: 3 / 4 ÷ 2 / 3 = 9 / 8

1. Familiarize with Number Properties:

Commutative Property: The order of numbers does not affect the result (applies to both addition and multiplication).

Associative Property: The grouping of numbers does not affect the result (also applies to both addition and multiplication).

Distributive Property: Expanding multiplication over addition or subtraction.

Identity Property: The sum of any number and zero is the number itself (for addition) and the product of any number and one is the number itself (for multiplication).

Inverse Property: Every number has an inverse such that their sum (for addition) or product (for multiplication) will yield the identity number.

Rational Numbers: Numbers that can be written as a fraction (quotient) of two integers.

Real Numbers: All numbers that can be plotted on a number line, including both rational and irrational numbers.

2. Familiarize with Number Properties:

Commutative Property: The order of numbers does not affect the result (applies to both addition and multiplication).

Associative Property: The grouping of numbers does not affect the result (also applies to both addition and multiplication).

Distributive Property: Expanding multiplication over addition or subtraction.

Identity Property: The sum of any number and zero is the number itself (for addition) and the product of any number and one is the number itself (for multiplication).

Inverse Property: Every number has an inverse such that their sum (for addition) or product (for multiplication) will yield the identity number.

Adding or Multiplying Odd and Even Numbers

What are the consistent patterns when you add or multiply odd and even numbers? Here are some established truths when dealing with the addition or multiplication of odd and even figures:

Keep these in mind:

The sum of two odd numbers is even.

The sum of two even numbers is even.

The sum of an odd and an even number is odd.

The product of two odd numbers is odd.

The product of two even numbers is even.

The product of an odd and an even number is even.

Factors are whole numbers that, when multiplied together, give another specific number without leaving any remainder.

Here is a list of common divisibility rules:

Divisible by	If
2	Last digit is 0, 2, 4, 6, or 8
3	Sum of digits is divisible by 3
4	Last 2 digits divisible by 4
5	Last digit is 0 or 5
6	Number is divisible by 2 and 3
8	Last 3 digits divisible by 8
9	Sum of digits is divisible by 9
10	Last digit is 0

Factoring

Factoring a number involves identifying all the whole numbers that can multiply to give that number. Generally, these factors are arranged in ascending order.

A practical approach to find the factors of a number is to begin with the number 1 and continue pairing it up with other numbers. The process can be stopped once you find a number that has already been identified in a previous pairing.

For instance, when determining the factors of 16:
1 and 16,
2 and 8,
4 and 4.
So, the factors of 16 are 1, 2, 4, 8, and 16.

Prime Factorization

Prime numbers are unique numbers greater than 1 that are divisible only by 1 and themselves. For instance, 23 is a prime number because only 1 and 23 divide it evenly.

Some prime numbers include:
1, 2, 3, 5, 7, 11, 13, 19, 37.

Prime factorization is the process of breaking down a number into its prime components. It's especially useful in determining the highest common factor or the lowest common multiple among numbers, but there are multiple methods to achieve those.

Patterns and Algebra

In this lesson, we will explore the foundational elements of Patterns and Algebra. This section will assess your grasp of concepts surrounding patterns, relations, functions, and the critical skill of algebraic reasoning. While it might seem a tad overwhelming at first, fear not! In this chapter, we've gathered all the vital knowledge you'll need, simplifying it to ensure your understanding. You've got this, and with our guidance, you'll be confidently tackling your math exam. Together, we're paving your way to teacher certification. Let's begin!

1. Relations and Functions:

A **relation** pairs elements from one set (called the domain) with elements from another set (called the range). Think of it as a set of ordered pairs.

A **function** is a special type of relation where each element from the domain is paired with exactly one element from the range.

2. Concrete Models:

Concrete models are tangible or physical representations.

For example, if you wanted to show a function of how many cookies you can buy with a certain amount of money, you could use actual cookies and coins to illustrate it.

3. Tables:

Tables present data in rows and columns.

A table can show a relation by listing input values (domain) and their corresponding output values (range).

For a **function**, make sure each input has only one corresponding output.

4. Graphs:

Graphs plot points on a coordinate plane.

For relations, simply plot all the ordered pairs.

For functions, the "vertical line test" is useful: if a vertical line crosses the graph at more than one point, it's NOT a function.

5. Symbolic Representations:

This often involves mathematical notation.

For example,
$f(x)=x^2$ is a symbolic representation of a function where the output is the square of the input.

6. Verbal Representations:

Simply describing the relation or function in words.

E.g., "For every 2 hours of study, a student's score increases by 5 points."

7. Real-World Applications:

Functions and relations exist everywhere!

Example: The relationship between hours worked and wages earned can be illustrated using all the above methods. If you work 8 hours at $10 per hour, your wage is $80. This can be shown with a table, graph, equation, and more.

Practice Scenario:
Imagine you're saving money for a new gadget. Each week, you save $20.

Concrete Model: Place 20 pennies in a jar for every week.

Table: List out the weeks (1, 2, 3, ...) and the total savings ($20, $40, $60, ...).

Graph: On a coordinate plane, plot the weeks on the x-axis and the amount saved on the y-axis. Connect the points to show your savings over time.

Symbolic Representation:
$S(w)=20w$ where S is the savings and w is the number of weeks.

Verbal Representation: "Each week, I save an additional $20 towards my gadget."

A **linear function** is a function whose graph is a straight line. The general form of a linear function is
$y=mx+b$, where m is the slope and b is the y-intercept.

Video lesson:

https://www.youtube.com/embed/ZmMBFx8r7g0?si=s92M
HOtlj0IRUJhU

Video lesson:

https://www.youtube.com/embed/QHeizWXeMgw?si=X77a
mqAWbOOvymw9

Video lesson:

https://www.youtube.com/embed/T-s9jiqGqxU?si=YXcmR
exedaLt08pv

1. Concrete Models:

Conceptualize with Physical Objects

Use a set of building blocks. If you stack one block for the first day, two for the second day, and so on, you're visually representing a linear function. The growth is consistent, just like the constant slope of a linear function.

2. Tables:

Tabulating Input and Output

x (input)	y (output)
0	b
1	m+b
2	2m+b
...	...

Notice how the difference in the y-values (outputs) remains consistent, which is a hallmark of linear functions.

Clarification on *consistency*: When we say the y-values are "consistent" in the context of a linear function, we're referring to the difference between successive y-values, not the y-values themselves. This difference remains constant, and it's precisely the slope m.

To illustrate with the table:
From x=0 to x=1:
Change in y = (m+b) - b = m

From x=1 to x=2:
Change in y = (2m+b) - (m+b) = m

As you can see, the difference between successive y-values (outputs) is consistently m, which is the slope of the linear function.

The y-values themselves indeed change, but the **rate of their change**—the difference between them—is what remains constant in a linear function. This consistent rate of change is the defining characteristic of linear functions.

3. Graphs:

Plotting the Linear Function
- Using graph paper or a graphing tool:
    - Plot the y-intercept (b).
    - Use the slope (m) to determine the next point. If m=2, for example, move up 2 units and to the right 1 unit from the y-intercept.
    - Draw a straight line connecting your points.
    - The graph should be a straight line, another key identifier of linear functions.

4. Symbolic Representations:

Understanding the Equation
- y=mx+b
- m: Slope. Indicates the steepness of the line. If positive, the line rises; if negative, it falls.
- b: y-intercept. The point where the line crosses the y-axis.

5. Verbal Representations:

Describing the Function in Words
- For each increase of 1 in x, y increases by m units.
- The graph intersects the y-axis at point (0, b).

Key Concepts to Remember:
- The slope (m) indicates how steep the line is. It represents the change in the y-value for a unit change in the x-value.
- The y-intercept (b) tells us where the line intersects with the y-axis.
- Linear functions exhibit a constant rate of change.

Alright, let's embark on understanding how to use algebraic concepts and reasoning to deepen our mathematical thinking. Here's a guide on how to utilize algebraic concepts for various tasks.

Video lesson:
https://www.youtube.com/embed/SxkKAp1s2Fg?si=X4Vk NenKgk8NWIVm

Video lesson:
https://www.youtube.com/embed/dJT8QyjWqxI?si=Lw2Mu
qkioYtlmZva

1. Investigating Patterns:

Algebraic Concepts: Variables, constants, sequences, series.

How to Use: Identify and represent patterns using variables. For instance, the arithmetic sequence $a_n = a_1 + (n-1)d$ describes a pattern where each term increases by a constant difference

2. Making Generalizations:

Algebraic Concepts: Expressions, equations, and formulas.

How to Use: Recognize common structures or properties and express them algebraically. For instance, for any even integer x, x^2 is also even.

3. Formulating Mathematical Models:

Algebraic Concepts: Equations, inequalities, functions.

How to Use: Translate real-world situations into algebraic expressions or equations. For example, if a car rental costs a flat fee f plus p dollars per mile driven, the total cost C for driving m miles is = + $C=f+pm$.

4. Making Predictions:

Algebraic Concepts: Functions, extrapolation.

How to Use: Use established patterns or models to forecast future events or values. Given a linear model for a growing plant's height, you can predict its height in future days.

5. Validating Results:

Algebraic Concepts: Equivalence, solution sets, algebraic manipulation.
How to Use:

- **Check Solutions**: Solve algebraically and substitute back into the original equation to verify.
- **Use Alternative Methods**: For a given problem, approach it using a different algebraic technique to see if results are consistent.
- **Logical Consistency**: Ensure results align with known properties. For instance, if solving for the sides of a triangle, the sum of the lengths of two sides should always be greater than the length of the third side.

Key Strategies and Tips:
Break Problems Down: When faced with a complex problem, break it into smaller, more manageable pieces. This often makes patterns more evident.

Visualize with Graphs: For many, visualizing a problem (like graphing a function) can make patterns, predictions, and validations clearer.

Practice Algebraic Manipulation: The more comfortable you are with manipulating algebraic expressions and equations, the easier it'll be to see patterns, make predictions, and validate results.

Contextual Understanding: Always try to understand the real-world implications or contexts of an algebraic representation. This can guide predictions and ensure results make logical sense.

Practice Scenario:

Imagine the population of a city has been growing linearly. In 2020, it was 50,000, and in 2022, it was 54,000.

Pattern: The population grows by 2,000 each year.

Generalization: The growth is linear, so the formula might be $P = 50{,}000 + 2{,}000(y - 2020)$, where P is the population and y is the year.

Mathematical Model: The linear equation above.

Prediction: Using the model, the predicted population for 2025 would be 60,000.

Validation: If in 2023, the city reports a population of 56,000, it aligns with our model, validating our formula and prediction.

Understanding the foundational algebraic concepts and honing your ability to apply them in these ways will not only boost your problem-solving skills but also equip you to tackle a wide range of mathematical challenges.

Understanding sequences and being able to describe and construct them using various methods is a critical topic for your math exam. Here's a breakdown:

Sequences: Overview

A **sequence** is an ordered list of numbers. Each number in a sequence is called a term. Sequences can follow a specific pattern or rule.

1. Verbal Descriptions of Sequences:

Describing a sequence in words.

E.g., "Starting at 3, each term is twice the previous term" describes a geometric sequence like 3, 6, 12, 24, ...

2. Numerical Representations of Sequences:

Lists or sets of numbers that represent the terms of the sequence.
E.g., An arithmetic sequence might be represented as 2, 5, 8, 11, ... where the common difference is 3.

3. Graphical Representations of Sequences:

Plotting the terms of a sequence on a graph.
Typically, the x-axis represents the position of the term in the sequence (1st, 2nd, 3rd, etc.), and the y-axis represents the value of the term.

An arithmetic sequence will appear as points on a straight line (if connected), whereas a geometric sequence might show exponential growth or decay.

4. Symbolic Representations of Sequences:

Using formulas or general expressions to describe sequences.

Arithmetic Sequence: $a_n = a_1 + (n-1)d$ where a_1 is the first term and d is the common difference.

Geometric Sequence: $a_n = a_1 \times r^{(n-1)}$ where a_1 is the first term and r is the common ratio.

Implicit vs. Explicit Rules:

Implicit Rules: These don't give the nth term directly but provide a relationship between terms. For instance, $a_n = a_{n-1} + 3$ tells you each term is 3 more than the previous term but doesn't directly give a formula for the nth term.

Explicit Rules: These provide a direct formula to find the nth term without needing to know other terms. The arithmetic and geometric sequence formulas above are examples of explicit rules.

Tips and Key Concepts:

Recursive vs. Closed Form: Recursive formulas (like the implicit rule above) define a sequence by relating a term to one or more previous terms. Closed form or explicit formulas (like the explicit rules) provide a direct way to find the nth term.

Recognizing Patterns: A significant part of dealing with sequences is recognizing their patterns. Whether you're given a verbal description, a list of numbers, a graph, or a formula, try to discern if it's arithmetic (constant difference), geometric (constant ratio), or some other type.

Using Graphs: When you graph a sequence, the behavior of the graph can often tell you about the nature of the sequence. For instance, a straight line suggests an arithmetic sequence, while a curve that consistently rises or falls suggests a geometric sequence.

Practice Scenario:

Consider the sequence described as "Starting from 4, each term is 3 times the previous one."

- **Verbal**: Given in the scenario.
- **Numerical**: 4, 12, 36, 108, ...
- **Graphical**: If plotted, this would show an upward curve (exponential growth).
- **Symbolic (Explicit Rule)**: $a_n = 4 \times 3^{(n-1)}$

Video lesson:

https://www.youtube.com/embed/eqpz9BzaGd4?si=Om-gg FzXXqJt0Kl7

Video lesson:

https://www.youtube.com/embed/RYDscpLcrk4?si=79uNM eug9wJoLGql

Let's dive into the properties, graphs, and applications of relations and functions, both linear and nonlinear, to ensure you have a comprehensive understanding for your exam.

Linear vs. Nonlinear Functions:

Linear Functions:

They produce a straight line when graphed.

Standard form: y=mx+b where m is the slope and b is the y-intercept.

Properties: Constant rate of change, represented by the slope m.

Nonlinear Functions:

These can be quadratic, cubic, exponential, logarithmic, etc.

They do not form straight lines when graphed.

E.g., Quadratic (parabola): $y = ax^2 + bx + c$

Graphs of Functions:

- Recognize the shape or curve associated with common functions (linear, quadratic, exponential, etc.).

- Identify key features:
  - X and Y Intercepts: Points where the graph crosses the x or y axis.
  - Maxima and Minima: Highest and lowest points on a curve.
  - Asymptotes: Lines that the graph approaches but never touches or crosses.

Properties of Linear and Nonlinear Functions:

Linear:

Slope (Rate of Change): Rise over run; the change in y for a unit change in x.

Y-intercept: The point where the line crosses the y-axis.

Nonlinear (e.g., Quadratic):

Vertex: The highest or lowest point on the parabola.

Axis of Symmetry: The vertical line that splits the parabola into two mirror images.

Applications in Mathematical & Real-World Situations:

Linear Functions:
- Predicting sales over time.
- Calculating cost based on production units.

Nonlinear Functions:
- Population growth (exponential function).
- Projecting the path of a thrown ball (quadratic function).

Analyzing, Modeling, and Solving Problems:

Analysis: Interpreting graphs, using properties of functions, and determining function types (linear, quadratic, etc.).

Modeling: Translating real-world problems into mathematical terms, often using functions to represent relationships.

Solving: Manipulating equations, using algebraic techniques, or graphically interpreting to find solutions.

Video lesson:

https://www.youtube.com/embed/3Uyqxh3ulHg?si=30a6H KRTAWDinZBd

Video lesson:

https://www.youtube.com/embed/CHuxHNuVRBE?si=WM B9T5Th1l_soM2g

Video lesson:

https://www.youtube.com/embed/uU5kGK4hTs0?si=XOi1F f16Z8DExRzu

Translating problem-solving situations into algebraic expressions and equations is a fundamental skill in mathematics, bridging the gap between real-world situations and abstract reasoning. Here's what you need to know for your exam:

1. Algebraic Expressions vs. Equations:

Algebraic Expression: A combination of variables, numbers, and operations. It represents a value but doesn't make a statement of equality. E.g., $5x + 7$.
Equation: Consists of two expressions separated by an equals sign, stating that both sides represent the same value. E.g., $5x + 7 = 27$.

2. Variables and Unknowns:

Variable: A letter or symbol representing an unknown quantity that can vary. E.g., x, y, z.

Unknown: A specific variable you're trying to solve for in a problem. In the equation $2x + 3 = 11$, x is the unknown.

3. Translating Words into Algebraic Expressions:

Common phrases and their algebraic equivalents:

"Sum of" means addition. E.g., "sum of a and b" is $a + b$.

"Difference between" means subtraction. E.g., "difference between a and b" is $a - b$.

"Product of" means multiplication. E.g., "product of a and b" is $a \times b$.

"Quotient of" means division. E.g., "quotient of a and b" is a / b.

"Increased by" or "more than" typically means addition.

"Decreased by" or "less than" typically means subtraction.

4. Formulating Equations from Word Problems:

Identify the Unknown: Determine what you're trying to find. If a problem asks for the age of Sam, let s represent Sam's age.

Translate Sentence by Sentence: Convert the problem's sentences into mathematical relationships. For example, "Sam is twice as old as Tom" can be written as $s = 2t$.

Ensure Consistency: Make sure your equations are consistent with the provided information.

5. Tips for Successful Translation:

Underline Key Information: This can help in identifying the critical parts of a word problem.

Sketch if Needed: For problems involving geometry or distances, a quick sketch might help in formulating equations.

Units: Always keep an eye on units (meters, kilograms, hours, etc.). They can provide clues about what operations to use.

Double-Check: Once you've translated a problem into an equation, review it to ensure it makes logical sense.

Practice Scenario:

Suppose a word problem says: "Sally has 5 more apples than John. Together they have 23 apples. How many apples does each person have?"

Translation:

Let j represent the number of apples John has.

Sally has $j + 5$.

Equation: $j + (j + 5) = 23$

Video lesson:
https://www.youtube.com/embed/do6fQFWrrOo?si=GBUk Na3gXFnobwLF

Translating problem-solving situations into algebraic expressions and equations is a fundamental skill in mathematics, bridging the gap between real-world situations and abstract reasoning. Here's what you need to know for your exam:

1. Algebraic Expressions vs. Equations:

Algebraic Expression: A combination of variables, numbers, and operations. It represents a value but doesn't make a statement of equality. E.g., 5x + 7.

Equation: Consists of two expressions separated by an equals sign, stating that both sides represent the same value. E.g., 5x + 7 = 27.

2. Variables and Unknowns:

Variable: A letter or symbol representing an unknown quantity that can vary. E.g., x, y, z.

Unknown: A specific variable you're trying to solve for a problem. In the equation 2x + 3 = 11, x is the unknown.

3. Translating Words into Algebraic Expressions:

Common phrases and their algebraic equivalents:

"Sum of" means addition. E.g., "sum of a and b" is a + b.

"Difference between" means subtraction. E.g., "difference between a and b" is a - b.

"Product of" means multiplication. E.g., "product of a and b" is a x b.

"Quotient of" means division. E.g., "quotient of a and b" is a / b.

"Increased by" or "more than" typically means addition.

"Decreased by" or "less than" typically means subtraction.

4. Formulating Equations from Word Problems:

Identify the Unknown: Determine what you're trying to find. If a problem asks for the age of Sam, let *s* represent Sam's age.

Translate Sentence by Sentence: Convert the problem's sentences into mathematical relationships. For example, "Sam is twice as old as Tom" can be written as s = 2t.

Ensure Consistency: Make sure your equations are consistent with the provided information.

5. Tips for Successful Translation:

Underline Key Information: This can help in identifying the critical parts of a word problem.

Sketch if Needed: For problems involving geometry or distances, a quick sketch might help in formulating equations.

Units: Always keep an eye on units (meters, kilograms, hours, etc.). They can provide clues about what operations to use.

Double-Check: Once you've translated a problem into an equation, review it to ensure it makes logical sense.

Practice Scenario:

Suppose a word problem says: "Sally has 5 more apples than John. Together they have 23 apples. How many apples does each person have?"

Translation:

Let j represent the number of apples John has.

Sally has $j + 5$.

Equation: $j + (j + 5) = 23$

Video lesson:

https://www.youtube.com/embed/2nhltdM2xUY?si=s3StT3 GRTipwlb2P

Proportional reasoning is a foundational concept in mathematics, enabling one to see relationships between quantities. Let's delve into the different methods to model and solve such problems.

1. Proportional Reasoning Basics:

Definition: Recognizing and using relationships between equivalent ratios.
Key Features: Constant rate of change and a linear relationship passing through the origin.

2. Concrete Methods:

Example: If 3 apples cost $6, using physical apples and coins can help model the situation and deduce that 1 apple costs $2.

3. Numeric Methods:

Direct Calculation: For a proportion like $\frac{a}{b} = \frac{c}{d}$, cross-multiply to solve for the unknown.
Unit Rate: Determine the amount for one unit (like price per item) to solve problems.

4. Tabular Methods:

Ratio Tables: List equivalent ratios in a table. If 2 pencils cost $3, a ratio table might show that 4 pencils cost $6, 6 pencils cost $9, and so on.

5. Graphic Methods:

Coordinate Graph: Plot the proportional relationship on a graph. Proportional relationships will always pass through the origin and form a straight line.

Tape Diagrams: Use segmented bars to represent and compare quantities.

6. Algebraic Methods:

Equations: Express the proportion as an equation (e.g., $y = kx$ where k is the constant of proportionality).

Solving for Unknowns: Use algebraic manipulation to determine the value of an unknown in a proportion.

7. Using Ratios and Percents with Fractions and Decimals:

Ratios: Express a relationship between two quantities. If there are 4 boys for every 5 girls, the ratio is 4:5.

Percents: A ratio out of 100. To convert a fraction or decimal to a percent, multiply by 100. E.g., 0.25 is 25%.

Conversion: Toggle between fractions, decimals, and percentages as needed for calculations. E.g., 75% is equivalent to 0.75 or ¾.

Practice Scenario:

Imagine you're baking cookies and have a recipe for 8 cookies but need to bake 20. If the recipe requires 2 cups of sugar for 8 cookies, how much sugar is needed for 20 cookies?

Solution: Set up a proportion. Let x be the amount of sugar for 20 cookies.

$$\frac{2 \text{ cups of sugar}}{8 \text{ cookies}} = \frac{x \text{ cups of sugar}}{20 \text{ cookies}}$$

Solving for x you'll find you need 5 cups of sugar for 20 cookies.

Applying Algebraic Methods to Whole Numbers Using Basic Operations

🔍 **Key Terms & Definitions:**

Whole Numbers: All non-negative numbers starting from 0, without any fractional or decimal parts.

Basic Operations: Addition (+), Subtraction (−), Multiplication (×), Division (÷).

Algebraic Methods: Using symbols, usually letters, to represent numbers and relationships between them.

📐 **Core Concepts:**

1. **Addition**: Combining two or more numbers.
   - E.g., if $a = 4$ and $b = 3$, $a + b = 7$.
2. **Subtraction**: Finding the difference between two numbers.
   - E.g., if $c = 9$ and $d = 5$, $c - d = 4$.
3. **Multiplication**: Finding the total of adding a number to itself multiple times.
   - E.g., if $x = 6$, $x \times 3 = 18$.
4. **Division**: Splitting a number into equal parts.
   - E.g., if $y = 21$, $y \div 3 = 7$.

📚 **Algebraic Representations**:

* **Symbols for Unknowns**: Letters (like x, y, a, b) represent unknown numbers.
* **Equations**: Mathematical statements that show the equality of two expressions.
  * E.g., $x + 5 = 9$.

✒️ **Practical Tips for Algebraic Operations:**

Inverse Operations: Addition and subtraction are inverses. Multiplication and division are inverses. Understanding this can help solve for unknowns.

Order of Operations: Remember PEMDAS/BODMAS: Parentheses/Brackets, Exponents/Orders, Multiplication & Division (from left to right), Addition & Subtraction (from left to right).

Check Your Work: Once you solve an equation, plug your answer back into the equation to ensure it's correct.

🌐 **Real-world Connections**:

* **Budgeting**: If you earn a dollars and spend b dollars, your savings are $a - b$.
* **Shopping**: Buying x items at y dollars each will cost $x \times y$ dollars.

Geometry and Measurement

Geometry and Measurement: The teacher understands concepts and principles of geometry and measurement.

Video lesson:
https://www.youtube.com/embed/Visr1DjNTmM?si=TE_E78hs82VuHeAV

Video lesson:
https://www.youtube.com/embed/oPzewkf42Us?si=4AHwuemdMKOUrD50

Video lesson:
https://www.youtube.com/embed/AiJdpmR8cm4?si=dqzRHAj-72wMTgqk

Video lesson:
https://www.youtube.com/embed/h0LNU2aj-Vg?si=llgcHH
9uymEg7MWf

Video lesson:
https://www.youtube.com/embed/-ddcJq9BHIo?si=JLCPe-f
4NWF_iXH2

Spatial Concepts in Geometry

1. Direction:

Definition: Direction refers to the path along which something moves, lies, or points.
Examples: North, South, East, West, left, right, up, down, etc.

Vectors: In mathematics and physics, a vector has both magnitude and direction, often represented by an arrow where the length represents magnitude and the direction of the arrow indicates direction.

2. Shape:

Definition: Shapes are forms such as circles, squares, triangles, etc.

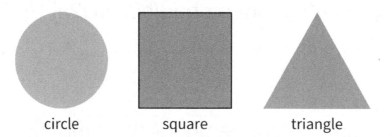

circle   square   triangle

2D Shapes: Have only two dimensions (length and width). (Examples above)

3D Shapes (Solids): Have three dimensions (length, width, and height).

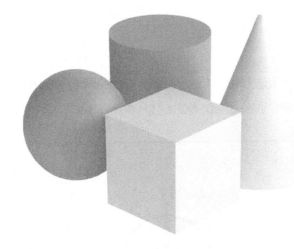

Examples: Sphere, Cube, Cylinder, Cone, Prism, Pyramid, etc.

Properties of Shapes: Area, perimeter (2D shapes); surface area, volume (3D shapes).

Video lesson:

https://www.youtube.com/embed/4dYjs-rORDA?si=2QpYVoMKDU7Ycjgi

Video lesson:

https://www.youtube.com/embed/ireCnPtSqAY?si=wOfv11CPG2dGPTml

3. Structure:

Definition: Structure refers to the arrangement and interrelationship of parts in a construction, which can be physical (like architecture) or abstract (like proofs in geometry).

Basic Structures in Geometry:

Lines: Can be straight or curved; have infinite length but no breadth.

Types:

- Line segments

Line Segment

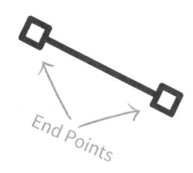

End Points

- Rays

Ray

When there is one end it is called a "Ray"

- Perpendicular lines

Perpendicular lines

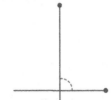

Two lines that intersect at a 90 degree angle

- Parallel lines

Parallel lines

Two lines that will never intersect

Angles: Formed when two lines meet.

Types: Acute, Right, Obtuse

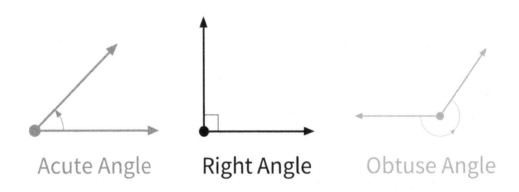

Acute Angle   Right Angle   Obtuse Angle

Triangles: Classified by side lengths (equilateral, isosceles, scalene) or angles (acute, right, obtuse).

Video lesson:
https://www.youtube.com/embed/YhKtxUOz3Cc?si=c8f5-d
W6mwTMeKj-

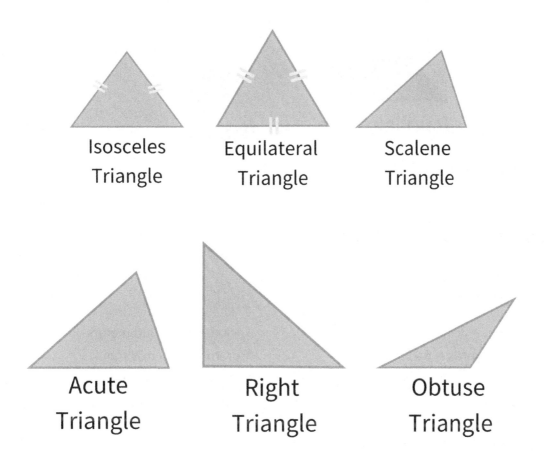

Quadrilaterals: Four-sided shapes.

Types: Square, Rectangle, Trapezium, Parallelogram, Rhombus.

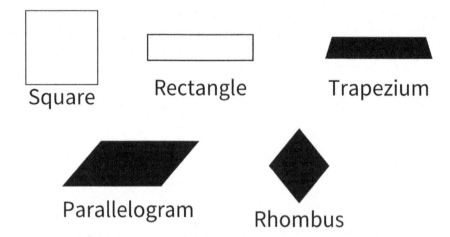

Square   Rectangle   Trapezium

Parallelogram   Rhombus

Measurement in Geometry

1. Conversions:

1 yard = 3 feet = 36 inches

1 mile = 1,760 yards = 5,280 feet

1 acre = 43,560 square feet

1 hour = 60 minutes

1 minute = 60 seconds

1 liter = 1000 milliliters = 1000 cubic centimeters

1 meter = 100 centimeters = 1000 millimeters

1 kilometer = 1000 meters

1 gram = 1000 milligrams

1 kilogram = 1000 grams

1 cup = 8 fluid ounces

1 pint = 2 cups

1 quart = 2 pints

1 gallon = 4 quarts

1 pound = 16 ounces

1 ton = 2,000 pounds

Metric numbers with four digits are presented without a comma (e.g., 9960 kilometers). For metric numbers greater than four digits, a space is used instead of a comma (e.g., 12 500 liters).

2. Measuring Formulas:

Formula Name	Formula
Perimeter of a Rectangle	$P = 2l + 2w$ (where l is length and w is width)
Perimeter of a Square	$P = 4s$ (where s is the side length)
Perimeter of a Triangle	$P = a + b + c$ (where a, b, and c are the sides)
Circumference of a Circle	$C = 2\pi r$ (where r is the radius)
Area of a Rectangle	$A = lw$
Area of a Square	$A = s^2$
Area of a Triangle	$A = \frac{1}{2}bh$ (where b is base and h is height)
Area of a Parallelogram	$A = bh$
Area of a Trapezoid	$A = \frac{1}{2}(a + b)h$ (where a and b are the bases)
Area of a Circle	$A = \pi r^2$
Volume of a Rectangular Solid	$V = lwh$
Volume of a Cube	$V = s^3$
Volume of a Sphere	$V = \frac{4}{3}\pi r^3$
Volume of a Cylinder	$V = \pi r^2 h$
Volume of a Square Based Pyramid	$V = \frac{1}{3}s^2 h$
Volume of a Right Circular Cone	$V = \frac{1}{3}\pi r^2 h$
Pythagorean Theorem	$a^2 + b^2 = c^2$ (where c is the hypotenuse)

Video lesson:

https://www.youtube.com/embed/Cqu0sD-XFUA?si=dlwfHkQBKB-jXk0U

Point, Line, Plane and Solid

- A Point has no dimensions, only position
- A Line is one-dimensional
- A Plane is two dimensional (2D)
- A Solid is three-dimensional (3D)

Tessellation

A tessellation (or tiling) involves arranging flat shapes on a surface without any spaces or overlaps.

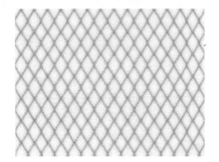

Rhombus
Tessellation

Fish
Tessellation

Hexagon and
Triangle
Tessellation

Measurement Concepts, Approximation, Estimation, and Effects of Error

1. Introduction

Measurement plays a crucial role in everyday life and is a foundational concept in mathematics. Understanding how to approximate and estimate measurements, and being aware of potential errors, is critical for accurate and meaningful results.

2. Key Concepts

Measurement

Definition: The process of determining the size, length, volume, area, or other attributes of an object.

Units: Always ensure that you're using the appropriate units for what you're measuring. For example, length might be measured in meters or feet, while volume might be measured in liters or gallons.

Approximation

Definition: A value or estimate that is nearly equal to the true value, but not exact.

Purpose: Useful when an exact number isn't necessary. For instance, if you're trying to determine if a room can hold 100 people, you might not need to know its exact area in square feet.

Video lesson:
https://www.youtube.com/embed/K26oJH8UhaQ?si=mX-EY4kFyBVTp0iw

Video lesson:
https://www.youtube.com/embed/959ICbiFHKU?si=CL-p3FHaXlv99OHJ

Video lesson:
https://www.youtube.com/embed/8Dge_yggkFQ?si=yVGzSs0QIHNckq1l

Estimation

Definition: Making an educated guess based on given information. It's often less detailed than a measured value.

Round Numbers: Estimations often involve round numbers. For example, estimating a grocery bill to be about $50 rather than $48.37.

Methods: Front-end estimation, rounding, clustering, compatible numbers, etc.

The Power of Estimation

Imagine effortlessly being able to:
- Predict the total of your grocery bill.
- Decide which product offers the best bang for your buck.
- Gauge sizes, spaces, and angles without a ruler.
- Swiftly estimate the number of attendees at a party, cars in a parking lot, books on a rack, or even birds in the sky.

It's not about pinpoint accuracy but making informed guesses that are "close enough" for practical purposes.

Precision vs. Practicality

In the world of mathematics:

🔍 Exactness is often paramount.

In daily life:

⚖ A few dollars might overshadow mere pennies. Prioritize the bigger picture!

What is Estimation?

Estimation is the art of approximating. It's not about nailing the perfect number but getting a number that's reasonably close.

The aim? A sensible answer without the wait!

Why Estimate?

$ Save Money: Before paying up, do a rapid estimate.

Example: Suppose you're buying six books priced at $2.85 each. Your bill is $18.90. Does that add up?

Quick Thought: "Six books at roughly $3 each is around $18."

⬤ **Time-Saver**: Skip exactness when close enough works.

Example: Planning to sow a flowerbed that's 64.5cm in length. If flowers are spaced 7cm apart, how many are required?

Quick Thought: "65cm is close to 70cm, and 70 divided by 7 is 10. So, I'd need about 10 plants."

🔍 Catch Calculator Errors: Estimation is your reality check.

Example: You're multiplying 113 by 47, but the calculator displays: 805.00.

Does that make sense?

Quick Thought: "113 times 47 is somewhat greater than 100 times 40, which is 4000."

Oops! A mistake must've slipped in. Always double-check.

Effects of Error on Measurement

Definition: Discrepancies between the measured value and the true value due to mistakes or limitations in measuring tools.

Types of Errors:

Systematic Errors: These are consistent and predictable. For example, a scale that always reads 5 grams too heavy.

Random Errors: These are unpredictable and can vary. For instance, errors due to human judgment.

Minimizing Errors: Always use appropriate tools, calibrate instruments regularly, double-check measurements, and train adequately.

Money in the United States

Overview of U.S. Currency

The United States uses the dollar as its standard unit of currency, symbolized by $. Both coins and paper bills are used, each with different denominations.

Penny: Value: $0.01 Depiction: Abraham Lincoln Material: Primarily Zinc with copper plating	
Nickel: Value: $0.05 Depiction: Thomas Jefferson Material: Cupro-Nickel alloy **Dime**: Value: $0.10 Depiction: Franklin D. Roosevelt Material: Cupro-Nickel alloy	

Dime:

Value: $0.10

Depiction: Franklin D. Roosevelt

Material: Cupro-Nickel alloy

Quarter:

Value: $0.25

Depiction: George Washington

Material: Cupro-Nickel alloy

Half Dollar:

Value: $0.50

Depiction: John F. Kennedy

Rarely used in everyday transactions

Dollar Coin:

Value: $1.00

Multiple designs, but the most recognized is the Sacagawea dollar.

Not commonly used in daily commerce

Paper Bills: Denominations and Key Figures

Note: Each bill showcases a prominent U.S. figure on one side and a significant landmark or event on the other.

$1: George Washington (Front), Great Seal of the U.S. (Back)

$2: Thomas Jefferson (Front), Signing of the Declaration of Independence (Back)

$5: Abraham Lincoln (Front), Lincoln Memorial with a depiction of Martin Luther King Jr.'s "I Have a Dream" speech (Back)

$10: Alexander Hamilton (Front), U.S. Treasury Building (Back)

$20: Andrew Jackson (Front), White House (Back)

$50: Ulysses S. Grant (Front), U.S. Capitol (Back)

$100: Benjamin Franklin (Front), Independence Hall (Back)

Concepts Relevant for Math Education

Making Change: Calculating the difference between the amount given and the total cost, then determining which combination of bills and coins to return.

Percentage Calculations: Understanding sales tax, discounts, and tips as they relate to money.

Decimal Operations: Adding, subtracting, multiplying, and dividing monetary amounts.

Word Problems: Creating and solving problems that involve transactions, savings, interests, and investments.

Practical Applications

Budgeting: Understanding income vs. expenses, planning for savings, and making informed financial decisions.

Interest & Compound Interest: The concept of earning money on savings or paying interest on loans.

Currency Conversion: Converting U.S. dollars to other currencies based on exchange rates, a useful concept especially in the context of global commerce.

Historical Context (Brief)

The U.S. adopted the dollar as its official currency with the Coinage Act of 1792. Over the years, there have been changes in the design, material, and denominations of both coins and paper bills, reflecting the nation's evolving history and values.

Video lesson:
https://www.youtube.com/embed/Wp0mA1JCIZU?si=E4Kh StGSBipSMqCX

Time

Basic Units of Time

Second (s): The base unit of time. It is defined by the International System of Units (SI) based on the duration of 9,192,631,770 periods of the radiation corresponding to the transition between two hyperfine levels of the ground state of the cesium-133 atom.

Minute (min): Consists of 60 seconds.
Hour (h): Made up of 60 minutes.
Day: Comprises 24 hours.
Week: Consists of 7 days.
Month: Duration varies, generally between 28 to 31 days.
Year: Roughly 365 days (366 in a leap year).

Longer Units of Time

Decade: 10 years.
Century: 100 years.
Millennium: 1,000 years.

Time on Clocks

Analog Clocks: These clocks have hour, minute, and sometimes second hands that rotate around a face.
Reading an analog clock requires understanding the divisions of the clock face and the relative lengths and speeds of the clock hands.
Digital Clocks: Display time numerically, often in hours:minutes (e.g., 14:30 or 2:30 PM).

Calculating Elapsed Time

Understanding the amount of time that has passed between two given times is essential. For example:
Starting time: 2:30 PM
Ending time: 5:15 PM
Elapsed time: 2 hours 45 minutes

Time Zones

The Earth is divided into multiple time zones, which impact time readings across different geographical locations. Knowing how to calculate time differences between zones is crucial, especially for activities like coordinating meetings or travel.

Leap Years and Calendar Calculations

A Leap Year occurs every four years to account for the roughly 365.25 days in a solar year. A leap year has 366 days, adding an extra day in February.
Understanding how to determine if a year is a leap year is important for accurate time calculations over multiple years.

Historical Context (Brief)

Time measurement has evolved from rudimentary sundials to atomic clocks with incredible precision. Different cultures have also had their calendars and methods of marking time, affecting our modern understanding and quantification of time.

Time Conversion Chart

Military Time	AM/PM Time
0000	12:00 AM
0100	1:00 AM
0200	2:00 AM
0300	3:00 AM
0400	4:00 AM
0500	5:00 AM
0600	6:00 AM
0700	7:00 AM
0800	8:00 AM
0900	9:00 AM

1000	10:00 AM
1100	11:00 AM
1200	12:00 PM
1300	1:00 PM
1400	2:00 PM
1500	3:00 PM
1600	4:00 PM
1700	5:00 PM
1800	6:00 PM
1900	7:00 PM
2000	8:00 PM
2100	9:00 PM
2200	10:00 PM
2300	11:00 PM
2400/0000	12:00 AM (Midnight - start of new day)

Video lesson:
https://www.youtube.com/embed/wBrWBO1uZl8?si=Fz8r7n988AmzheUv

Translations, Rotations, Reflections, and Their Properties

Introduction

In geometry, figures can undergo specific movements or transformations. The primary rigid transformations are translations, rotations, and reflections. These transformations can help illustrate similarities, congruences, and symmetries of figures.

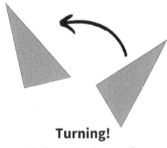

Turning!
This is called rotation

Flipping!
This is called reflection

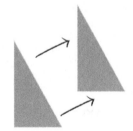

Slidding!
This is called traslation

Translations

Definition: A translation moves every point of a figure the same distance in the same direction.

Properties:
- Does not change the figure's size or shape.
- Results in a congruent figure.
- Preserves distances and angle measures.

Similarity and Congruency: When a figure is translated, the result is a figure that is congruent (same size and shape) to the original.

- The two figures must match in size to be considered congruent.
- If we have to adjust the size of one figure to match another, they are termed as Similar.

If we only ... Then the figures are ...

... Rotate, Reflect, or Translate →
Congruent

... additionally adjust the size →
Similar

Rotations

Definition: A rotation turns a figure around a fixed point called the center of rotation.
- **Properties**: Preserves size and shape of the figure.
- Maintains congruency.
- Angle of rotation determines how far the figure turns, measured in degrees.
- Direction (clockwise or counterclockwise) is also vital.

Illustration of Symmetry: Rotational symmetry is when a figure can be rotated less than 360° and still look the same. The number of positions in which it looks identical gives the order of rotational symmetry.

Reflections

Definition: A reflection flips a figure over a line, producing a mirror image.
- Properties: The line of reflection acts as the mirror.
- Each point of the original figure and its image are equidistant from the line.
- Preserves size and shape.
- Results in a congruent figure.

Illustration of Symmetry: Line of symmetry (or reflectional symmetry) exists if a figure can be reflected over a line so that the image coincides with the original figure. Many shapes, like rectangles, circles, and some triangles, have lines of symmetry.

Combined Transformations

Figures can undergo a combination of translations, rotations, and reflections. The order in which these transformations are applied can affect the resulting figure.

Video lesson:
https://www.youtube.com/embed/zRzv1znrQ0c?si=dIVhjH1Hmt9wvdAz

Congruency and Similarity

Congruent Figures: Figures that have the same size and shape. Rigid transformations (translations, rotations, reflections) will produce congruent figures.

Similar Figures: Figures that have the same shape but may have different sizes. They have proportional side lengths and congruent angles.

Note: While translations, rotations, and reflections result in congruent figures, other transformations like dilation can produce similar figures.

Tips for Success:

Visualization: Practice with tools such as tracing paper or digital platforms to understand how figures transform.

Hands-on Practice: Physically manipulate shapes (like on a coordinate grid) to understand transformations better.

Real-world Connections: Recognize these transformations in art, architecture, and nature to deepen understanding.

Video lesson:

https://www.youtube.com/embed/iKwWbeaJNol?si=jAmSZ aVPm7zLictS

Logical Reasoning, Justification, And Proof Within The Context Of Geometry's Axiomatic Structure

Axiomatic Structure of Geometry

Geometry as we know it today is based on the **axiomatic system**. This system starts with undefined terms (terms that we accept without a formal definition, such as points, lines, and planes) and from them, we derive definitions. Using these definitions and axioms (or postulates), which are accepted truths, we prove theorems.

Basic Components:

Undefined Terms: Fundamental entities that don't require a definition. For instance, in Euclidean geometry, the point, line, and plane are undefined.

Axioms/Postulates: Statements we accept without proof. E.g., "Through any two distinct points, there is exactly one line."

Theorems: Statements that are proven based on axioms, postulates, or previously proven theorems.

Logical Reasoning

Logical reasoning is a way to derive a conclusion from certain premises using rules of logic. This process is central to mathematical arguments.

Types of Reasoning:

- **Deductive Reasoning**: Starts with general premises and moves to specific conclusions. All theorems in geometry are proven using deductive reasoning.
- **Inductive Reasoning**: Based on patterns or examples. E.g., observing that the sun rises every day and deducing that it will rise tomorrow.

Justification and Proof

A proof is a logical argument demonstrating that a statement is true. Each step of the argument follows logically from the previous step, and every step is justified.

Types of Proofs in Geometry:

Two-column Proofs: A structured format where each step is listed in one column and its justification in the next.

Paragraph Proofs: Theorems are written as structured pieces of text.

Flow Proofs: Visual representations using shapes connected with arrows to show the logical flow of the argument.

Geometric Relationships and Their Proofs

Key Concepts and Proofs:

Parallel and Perpendicular Lines: Using axioms and the properties of transversals, we can prove angles as alternate interior, corresponding, or vertical, leading to the conclusion about parallelism.

Triangles: Concepts like congruence (SSS, SAS, ASA, AAS, and HL), similarity (AA, SAS, and SSS), Pythagoras theorem, and properties of special triangles.

Circles: Tangents, secants, arcs, and angles subtended by arcs form the basis for many theorems.

Transformations: Translation, reflection, and rotation can establish the congruence or similarity of figures.

Tips for Developing Proofs:

- **Understand the Given Information**: What are you starting with?

- **Understand the Desired Conclusion**: Where are you trying to go?

- **Draw a Diagram**: Helps visualize relationships.

- **Look for Auxiliary Lines**: Sometimes adding a line or point can simplify the proof.

- **Stay Logical and Sequential**: Each step should logically follow from the previous.

Polygons

A **polygon** is a closed, two-dimensional shape formed by a finite sequence of straight line segments connected end to end to form a closed circuit. The line segments that form a polygon are called its edges or sides, and the points where they meet are the polygon's vertices. Polygons can have any number of sides, but they must have at least three sides. The simplest polygon is the triangle, which has three sides.

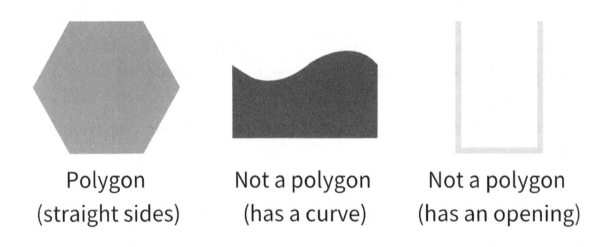

| Polygon | Not a polygon | Not a polygon |
| (straight sides) | (has a curve) | (has an opening) |

Did you know:

Polygon comes from Greek. Poly- means "many" and -gon means "angle".

Types of Polygons

Regular and Irregular

A regular polygon has all sides and all angels equal. If this isn't the case it's irregular.

A square is a
regular polygon

A rectangle is an
irregular polygon

Concave or Convex

A **convex polygon** does not have any angles that point inward. Specifically, every internal angle in a convex polygon is less than or equal to 180°.

Conversely, if a polygon has even one internal angle exceeding 180°, it is termed **concave**. (Remember: concave resembles having a "dent" or "cave" inside it.)

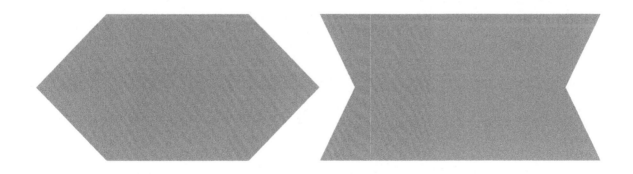

Convex

Concave

Properties of Regular Polygons

The **exterior angle** of a shape is formed by one of its sides and the extension of an adjacent side.

All exterior angles of a polygon sum up to 360°. Hence, each individual exterior angle is equal to 360° divided by n (where n is the number of sides/angles).

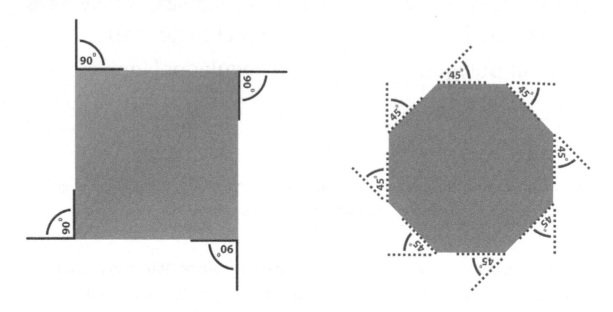

The **interior and exterior angles** are derived from the same straight line, so their combined measure is 180°.

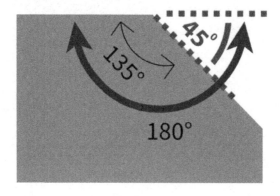

Video lesson:

https://www.youtube.com/embed/_NJ49q10N4c?si=_a9w0pmGSTpLaWTn

Finding Areas in Triangles

By dissecting regular polygons into triangles, we can derive some interesting insights:

Take note:

- The triangle's base corresponds to one side of the polygon.
- The triangle's height is equivalent to the polygon's "apothem."
- The area of a triangle is calculated as half the product of its base and height, thus:

Area of a single triangle = side × apothem ÷ 2

To determine the area of the entire polygon, sum up the areas of all these triangles (there are "n" triangles):

Polygon's Area = n × side × apothem ÷ 2

Considering the perimeter is the sum of all sides, which is n × side, we can conclude:

Polygon's Area = perimeter × apothem ÷ 2

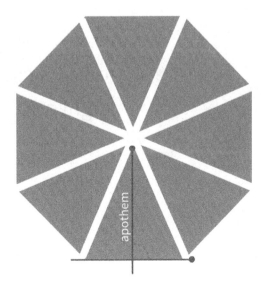

Perimeter and Area

The **perimeter** of a shape describes the length of its outer edge. It's a linear measure and thus will have units like:

- yards (yd.)
- meters (m)
- kilometers (km)
- millimeters (mm)

Area, on the other hand, signifies the total surface space enclosed by a shape. As it accounts for both length and width (or length × length for squares), its units are squared:

- square yards (yd.^2)
- square meters (m^2)
- square millimeters (mm^2)
- square feet (ft.^2)

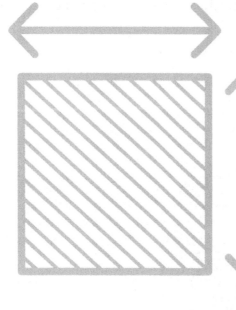

Perimeter is the length of all sides added together.

Area is the space inside (found by multiplying the height and width).

Finding The Area Of Irregular Shapes

Perimeter:

3 + 3 + 5 + 5 + 4 = 20 cm

Area:

Triangle= 1/2 x 4 x 1 = 2 cm^2

Rectangle= 4 x 5 = 20 cm^2

Total area: 22 cm^2

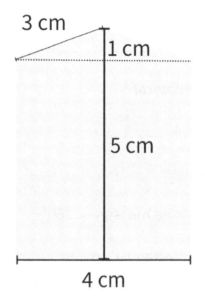

Video lesson:
https://www.youtube.com/embed/nqHxJXvAKWs?si=uSPv6uyex94hE_6w

Polygon Attributes

Triangle	
Sides: 3 Attributes: Total angle measure = 180°	 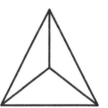

Types based on angles: acute, obtuse, right

Types based on sides: scalene, isosceles, equilateral

Quadrilateral

Sides: 4

Attributes:

Total angle measure = 360°

Types: rectangle, square, parallelogram, rhombus, trapezoid, kite

Attributes vary based on type (e.g., all angles of a rectangle are 90°)

Pentagon

Sides: 5

Attributes:

Total angle measure = 540°

Regular pentagon: all sides and angles are equa

Hexagon

Sides: 6

Attributes:

Total angle measure = 720°

Regular hexagon: all sides and angles are equal

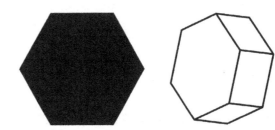

Heptagon (or Septagon)

Sides: 7

Attributes:

Total angle measure = 900°

Regular heptagon: all sides and angles are equal

Octagon

Sides: 8

Attributes:

Total angle measure = 1080°

Regular octagon: all sides and angles are equal

Decagon

Sides: 10

Attributes:

Total angle measure = 180° × (10 - 2) =
1440°

Regular decagon: all sides and angles
are equal, with each angle being 144°
(since 1440° ÷ 10 = 144°)

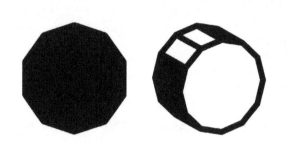

Coordinate Plane

A **coordinate plane** is a two-dimensional flat surface defined by two number lines: the x-axis, which is horizontal, and the y-axis, which is vertical. These axes intersect at a point called the origin. Every point on the coordinate plane can be identified by an ordered pair of numbers (x, y), where "x" is the distance from the y-axis (often called the x-coordinate) and "y" is the distance from the x-axis (often called the y-coordinate). The coordinate plane is used to plot points, lines, and curves in two-dimensional space.

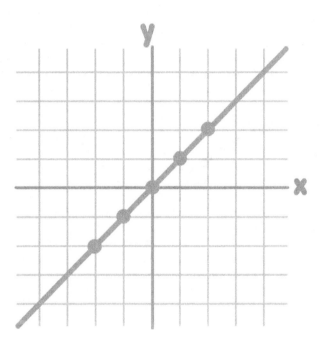

Cartesian Coordinates

In this system, we mark a **point** on the graph to show a specific location by moving left or right on the horizontal axis, called the **x-axis.** We can also move up or down the **y-axis**.

In the image below, the plot circled in red is located at the coordinates (0,0), which is called the origin.

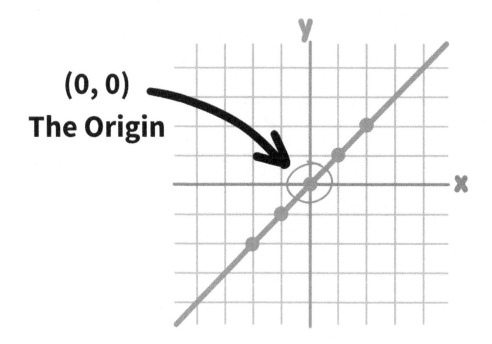

Writing Coordinates

Coordinates follow a specific sequence:

1. first the horizontal measurement (on the x axis),
2. followed by the vertical measurement (on the y axis).

This sequence is termed an **"ordered pair"** (two numbers with a designated sequence).

Typically, these numbers are distinguished by a comma and enclosed within brackets. If x becomes larger, the point shifts more to the right.
If x becomes smaller, the point shifts more to the left.

When y grows, the point ascends.
If y diminishes, the point descends.

Four Quadrants

The coordinate plane is divided into 4 quadrants, or sections of the plane.

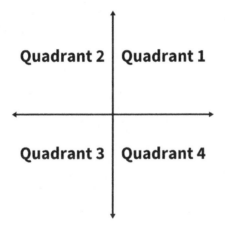

Then, we can also look at how the numbers, when plotted, are shown in the corresponding quadrants. Let's look at examples in the image below:

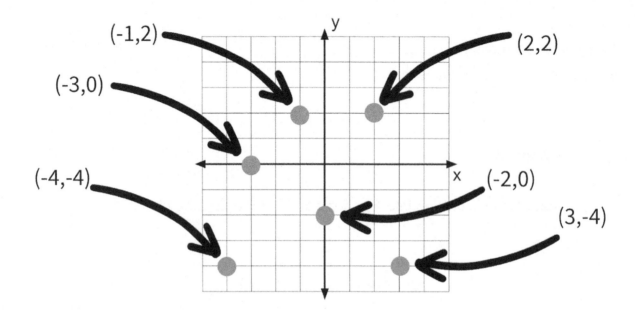

Probability and Statistics

Video lesson:
https://www.youtube.com/embed/vXH3eNYK6to?si=Z9Xs
KZpRdY26csRy

Data Analysis

There are lots of ways to represent data. For your exam, you'll need to be able to use numerical or graphical representations to analyze problems. The expectation is that teachers are able to represent numeric data graphically, including using **dot plots**, **stem-and-leaf plots**, **histograms**, and **box plots**. Let's cover this now:

Dot Plot

A way to display data using dots.

The dot plot to the right shows the popularity of breakfast choices.

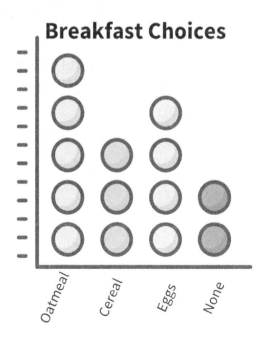

Breakfast Choices

Oatmeal Cereal Eggs None

Stem-and-Leaf Plot

Example: High jump contest

Bill's high jump results:

23, 25, 27, 36, 40

Stem-and-leaf plot:

Stem	Leaf
2	3, 5, 7
3	6
4	0

A graphical representation that organizes numerical data by separating each value into a "stem" (leading digits) and a "leaf" (final digit).

Histogram

A **histogram** is a graphical representation of data using bars of varying heights to illustrate the frequency of numerical intervals.

A histogram is like a bar graph, but it clusters numbers into **a range** of specific intervals, with the height of each bar indicating the count within that interval, and you get to choose the intervals!

Histogram example

There are 30 students in your class. You collect all of their math exam results, which vary from 40% to 100% correct.

The results are shown to the right:

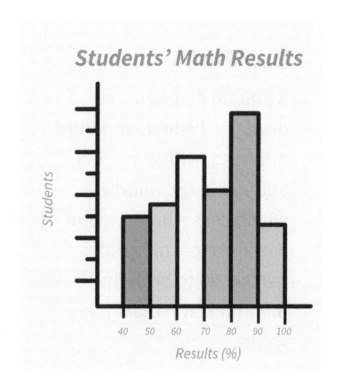

Bar Graph vs. Histogram

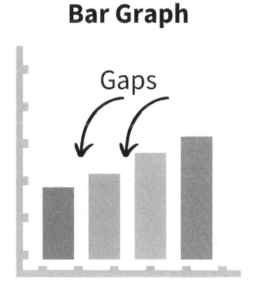

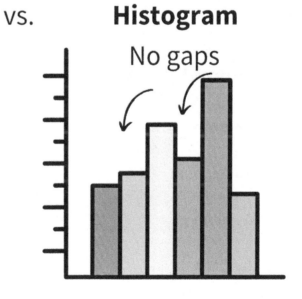

Box Plot

A unique diagram that displays the first, and third quartiles, with a median amount in the middle, which uses a box(es), and has lines reaching out (whiskers) to both the minimum and maximum values.

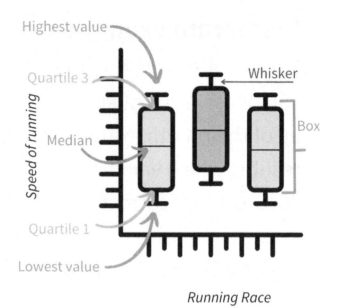

Running Race

A **line graph** is a chart that uses lines to connect individual data points, typically displaying trends over a period of time.

Snowfall Table

Month	Inches
November	18
December	26
January	23
February	18
March	13

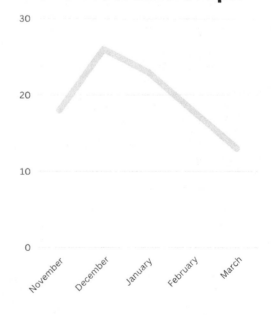

Pie Chart

A **pie chart** is a circular graph that represents data as slices of a pie, with each slice corresponding to a proportion or percentage of the whole.

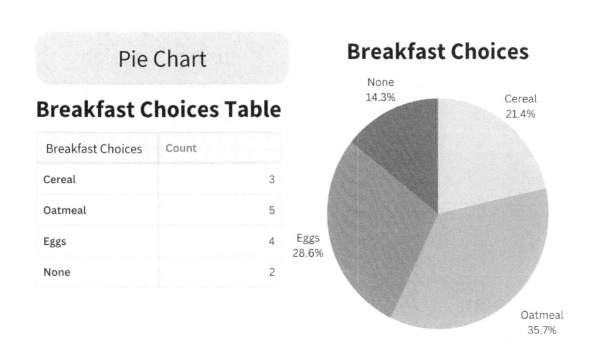

Pie Chart

Breakfast Choices Table

Breakfast Choices	Count
Cereal	3
Oatmeal	5
Eggs	4
None	2

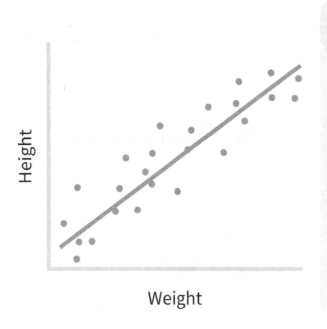

Weight

Scatter Plot

A graph that displays individual data points using Cartesian coordinates to represent values of two variables.

Video lesson:
https://www.youtube.com/embed/IBlylvPR508?si=nR5j5N
D-R4wMLI7x

Mean, Median, Mode, And Range

Mean

The **mean** is the average of the numbers, and we find the mean by adding up all the numbers and dividing by the amount of numbers that were added.

Example:

The mean of 3, 12, 21 is 12:

To find the answer, we added 3 + 12 + 21, which equals 36. Then, we divide 36 by 3, because there are a total of 3 numbers, which gives us 12.

Median

The **median** is found in the middle of the sorted list of numbers.

Example:

The median of 3, 12, 21 is 12.

To find the answer, we first need to make sure that all the numbers are placed in order from smallest to largest. In this case, that order is 3, 12, 21. Then, we find the number in the middle, and that is the median!

Finding the median when two numbers are in the middle

If you are asked to find the median when you find two numbers in the middle, this is what you do - let's learn by example!

3, 12, 14, 21.

1. Make sure the numbers are in order.
2. Identify the two numbers in the middle. In this case, it is 12 and 14.
3. Then, add the two numbers together: 12 + 14 = 26
4. Finally, divide the sum by two: 26 / 2 = 13.
5. The median of 3, 12, 14, and 21 is 13.

Mode

The **mode** is the number which appears most often.

Example:

The mode of 1, 2, 4, 4, 7, 7, 7, 9 = 7.

To find this, we simply identify the number that is present the most times.

Having more than one mode

What happens if two numbers appear the most often, but the same amount of times?

Well that's called **bimodal.**

Here's an example:

1, 2, 4, 4, 4, 7, 7, 7, 9

In this case, we'd have two modes: 4 and 7.

If you have more than two modes, that's called **multimodal**. Here's an example:
1, 1, 1, 2, 4, 4, 4, 7, 7, 7, 9
In this case, our modes are: 1, 4, and 7.

Range

The **Range** is the difference from the lowest and highest numbers.
For example:
The range between 1, 1, 1, 2, 4, 4, 4, 7, 7, 7, 9 = 8.
We find this by taking 9 (the highest number) subtracted by 1 (the lowest number).

Video lesson:
https://www.youtube.com/embed/Ba-Wwo0-Dc8?si=IIXPr_7CK4SXl81L

Video lesson:
https://www.youtube.com/embed/AMpSefKif2w?si=tTACfuU3qF-aWWgq

Exploring Concepts of Probability

1. Introduction to Probability

Definition: Probability is a measure of the likelihood of an event to occur. It's expressed as a number between 0 and 1 (or 0% to 100%).

Fundamental Principle: The probability of all possible outcomes of an experiment is equal to 1 (or 100%).

2. Key Probability Terminology

Experiment: A process that leads to one of several possible outcomes.

Outcome: The result of a single trial of an experiment.

Event: A specific outcome or combination of outcomes.

Sample Space (S): The set of all possible outcomes.

3. Basic Probability Formulas

P(E): Probability of event E occurring.

Formula: P(E) = Number of favorable outcomes / Total number of outcomes in the sample space.

4. Data Collection in Probability

Surveys and Polls: Useful for collecting large amounts of data quickly.

Observational Studies: Watch and record outcomes without interfering.

Experiments: Controlled methods where researchers manipulate one variable to discover an effect.

5. Probability Experiments

Simple Random Experiments: Experiments like tossing a coin or rolling a die.

Compound Experiments: Combining two or more simple random experiments, e.g., tossing two coins.

6. Simulations

Definition: A model of a real-world situation, often run on computers, to predict probable outcomes.

Importance: Simulations can be useful when real-world experiments are costly, dangerous, or time-consuming.

Examples: Tossing a virtual coin, simulating raindrops on a field to determine likelihood of a certain amount of rainfall.

7. Theoretical vs. Experimental Probability

Theoretical Probability: Based on the possible outcomes mathematically. (e.g., getting a head when flipping a coin is 1/2)

Experimental Probability: Based on actual experiments. (e.g., flipping a coin 100 times and getting 60 heads gives an experimental probability of 0.6 or 60%).

8. Law of Large Numbers

As more trials of a random experiment are conducted, the experimental probability approaches the theoretical probability.

9. Compound Events and Probability

Independent Events: The outcome of one event doesn't affect the outcome of another. (e.g., flipping a coin and rolling a die)

Dependent Events: The outcome of one event affects the outcome of another. (e.g., drawing two cards from a deck without replacement)

10. Conditional Probability

Probability of an event given that another event has already occurred.

Formula: $P(A|B) = P(A \text{ and } B) / P(B)$

Video lesson:
https://www.youtube.com/embed/IGQf3X4-ZDg?si=ahRvjg hThMQ-gKbW

Understanding Probability: Simple and Compound Events

Simple Events

Definition: Events that involve a single outcome.

Example: Rolling a die and getting a 4.

Compound Events

Definition: Combines two or more simple events.

Two Types: Independent and Dependent events.

Independent Events

Definition: Occurrence of one event does not affect the occurrence of the other.

Formula: $P(A \text{ and } B) = P(A) \times P(B)$

Example: Flipping a coin (event A) and rolling a die (event B).

Dependent Events

Definition: Occurrence of one event affects the occurrence of the other.

Formula: P(A and B) = P(A) × P(B|A)

Example: Drawing two cards from a deck without replacement.

Mutual Exclusivity

Definition: Two events cannot occur at the same time.

Formula for Either Event Occurring: P(A or B) = P(A) + P(B)

Note: For non-mutually exclusive events, the formula is P(A or B) = P(A) + P(B) - P(A and B).

Conditional Probability

Definition: The probability of an event occurring given that another event has already occurred.

Formula: P(A|B) = P(A and B) / P(B)

Using Combinations and Permutations in Probability

Combinations: When the order of selection does NOT matter.

Permutations: When the order of selection DOES matter.

Utilize combinations and permutations to determine the total number of possible outcomes for compound events.

Law of Total Probability

- Used when our sample space is divided into several disjoint events.
- Helps to find the probability of an event by considering all the ways that event could happen.

Complementary Events

Definition: The event that represents everything not in event A.

Formula: P(Not A) = 1 - P(A)

Video lesson:
https://www.youtube.com/embed/GPpccb7Cg00?si=wL8S 1-7Fb50Zzi5w

Determining Probabilities: Constructing Sample Spaces

1. Introduction to Sample Spaces

Sample Space (S): The set of all possible outcomes of an experiment or event.
Example: Rolling a die has a sample space S = {1, 2, 3, 4, 5, 6}.

2. Simple Events in a Sample Space

Simple Event: Represents a single outcome in the sample space.
Example: Drawing a single card from a deck (e.g., King of Hearts).

3. Constructing Sample Spaces

Listing Method: Write out all possible outcomes. Useful for experiments with few outcomes.

Tree Diagram: A branching diagram that represents all possible outcomes, often used for sequential events.

Venn Diagram: Used to represent and visualize sets, especially when events can overlap.

4. Events and Subsets

Any collection of outcomes (including individual outcomes) from the sample space is called an event.

Subset: A part of the sample space.
Example: If S = {1, 2, 3, 4}, then {1, 3} is a subset/event of S.

5. Equally Likely Outcomes

Outcomes in a sample space are equally likely when they have the same probability of occurring.

Example: Each side of a fair die has a 1/6 probability of landing face up.

6. Finding Probability Using Sample Spaces

Formula: P(E) = Number of favorable outcomes (for E) / Total number of outcomes in the sample space.

Ensure that all outcomes in your sample space are unique and exhaustive.

7. Compound Events

Definition: An event made up of two or more simple events.

To determine the sample space for compound events, consider all possible outcomes for each event and combine them.

Example: Tossing two coins yields the sample space S = {HH, HT, TH, TT}.

8. Using Sample Spaces for Multiple Steps

For multi-step experiments, determine the sample space for each step and then combine them.

Example: Choosing a card, replacing it, then choosing another has a sample space of 52×52.

9. Sample Spaces and Dependence

Remember, if the outcome of one event impacts another, they're dependent events. Adjust your sample space accordingly.

Example: Drawing two cards without replacement reduces the sample space for the second draw.

10. Challenges with Large Sample Spaces

Some experiments have large or infinite sample spaces (e.g., drawing a random point from a line segment).

In such cases, employ concepts of geometric probability or use bins/buckets to group outcomes.

Video lesson:
https://www.youtube.com/embed/acdKaKtFF7Y?si=ll_5xG 96PHNEHRyK

Probability using Combinations and Geometric Probability

Formula: $P(E) = \dfrac{\text{Number of favorable outcomes}}{\text{Total number of outcomes}}$

Combinations

Combinations: It's the selection of items from a larger pool, where the order of selection does not matter.
Formula for Combinations:

$$C(n, r) = \frac{n!}{r! \times (n-r)!}$$

- Where *n* is the total number of items and *r* is the number of items to choose.

Geometric Probability

Geometric probability involves geometric measures like length, area, and volume. The probability of an event E happening is given by:

$$P(E) = \frac{\text{Measure of event E}}{\text{Measure of the sample space}}$$

Probability as the Ratio of Two Areas

- Used mostly in 2D space (like on a plane).
- The probability of a specific region being selected is the ratio of its area to the total area.

Example Problem 1 (Combinations):

Question: In a class of 10 students, how many ways can a committee of 2 students be formed?

Solution:

Using the formula for combinations:

$$C(10, 2) = \frac{10!}{2! \times 8!} = 45 \text{ ways.}$$

Example Problem 2 (Geometric Probability):

Question: On a square dartboard of side 10 units, a circular region with radius 4 units is painted. If a dart hits the board at a random point, what is the probability it lands inside the circle?

Solution:

Area of square = $10 \times 10 = 100$ sq. units.

Area of circle = $\pi \times 4^2 = 16\pi$ sq. units.

Probability = $\frac{\text{Area of circle}}{\text{Area of square}} = \frac{16\pi}{100}$ or 0.16π.

Video lesson:

https://www.youtube.com/embed/6i48P8woQD4?si=sXYrzs0DcHjMKsUl

Video lesson:

https://www.youtube.com/embed/ekugNqRiKWE?si=xjvaK08OQbn0vPRk

Normal Distribution

As mathematicians, we can distribute or *give out* data in a variety of ways.

Sometimes data appears to be increasing, decreasing, or is in all sorts:

increasing

decreasing

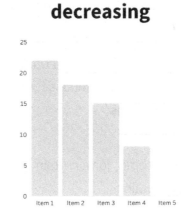

all over the place!

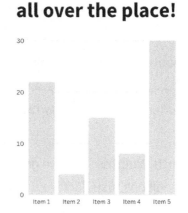

And other times, it appears like the data gets close to a **"Normal Distribution"** such as:

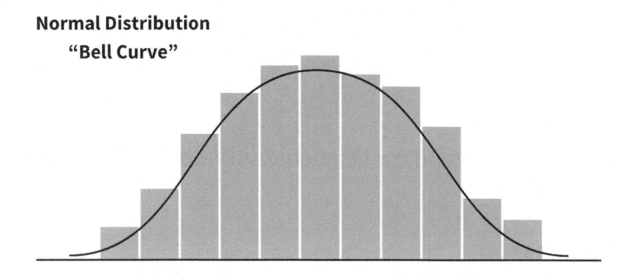

**Normal Distribution
"Bell Curve"**

Our curve above is called a Normal Distribution. This is often referred to as a "Bell Curve," because it looks like a bell.

Areas that often follow the bell curve:

Human Heights: In a large enough population, the distribution of people's heights tends to follow a normal distribution, with most people having heights around the average, and fewer people being either much shorter or much taller.

IQ Scores: Intelligence Quotient (IQ) scores are designed to follow a bell curve, with the majority of people scoring around the average of 100 and fewer people at the extreme ends.

Exam Scores: In a large class, if an exam is neither too easy nor too hard, the distribution of scores might resemble a bell curve, with most students scoring near the mean and fewer students receiving very high or very low scores.

Birth Weights: The weights of babies at birth, for a certain gestational age and under standard conditions, usually follow a normal distribution.

Measurement Errors: In many scientific experiments, random errors (due to unpredictable fluctuations) often follow a normal distribution around the true value.

Key Features of Normal Distribution

Mean (μ): The center of the distribution.
Standard Deviation (σ): Measures the spread or dispersion. The larger the standard deviation, the wider the bell curve.
Approximately 68% of the data falls within one standard deviation, 95% within two, and 99.7% within three.

Standard Normal Distribution:

A special case with a mean (μ) of 0 and a standard deviation (σ) of 1.

Any normal distribution can be transformed into this standard form using the formula: $Z = (X - \mu) / \sigma$

The **Z-score** indicates how many standard deviations a data point (X) is from the mean.

Making Inferences:

With a known mean and standard deviation, you can infer the probability of a particular outcome.
Use Z-tables or calculators to find the area under the curve, representing probabilities.

Practical Applications:

Percentiles: Find what percentage of the data falls below a particular value.

Confidence Intervals: Determine a range where a population parameter is likely to lie.

Hypothesis Testing: Assess if a sample could have come from a specific population.

 Congrats!

You have reached the end of this study guide! If it has helped you prepare, please share your testimonial using the URL below!

https://forms.gle/kMdyWGMk9WLew962A

We are wishing you all the best in passing your teacher certification exam, and progressing through your teaching career!

TeacherPreps Team

Made in United States
Orlando, FL
14 May 2025

61289030R00096